THE OUTER PLANETS
URANUS, NEPTUNE and PLUTO

Sh
S0135 J523 4

Exploring the Planets

THE OUTER PLANETS
URANUS, NEPTUNE and PLUTO

Duncan Brewer

CHERRYTREE BOOKS

A Cherrytree Book

Designed by Graham Beehag

First published by Marshall Cavendish Corporation 1992

This edition first published 1992
by Cherrytree Press Ltd
a subsidiary of
The Chivers Company Ltd
Windsor Bridge Road
Bath, Avon BA2 3AX

Copyright © Marshall Cavendish Corporation 1992

British Library Cataloguing in Publication Data

Brewer, Duncan
   The outer planets : Uranus, Neptune, Pluto
   1. Planets
   I. Title
   523.4

ISBN 0-7451-5133-7

Printed in Singapore by Times Offset Pte Ltd.

All rights reserved. No part of this publication may be reproduced, stored in a retrieval system, or transmitted, in any form or by any means without the prior permission in writing of the publisher, nor be otherwise circulated in any form of binding or cover other than that in which it is published and without a similar condition including this condition being imposed on the subsequent purchaser.

SAFETY NOTE

Never look directly at the Sun, either with the naked eye or with binoculars or a telescope. To do so can result in permanent blindness.

Acknowledgement

Most of the photographs, maps and diagrams in this book have been kindly supplied by NASA. The integral annotations use American spellings and imperial measurements.

Title Page Picture:
An artist's concept of the planet Uranus and its rings.

Contents

Uranus	6
Musical Astronomer	7
The Curious Comet	8
Gas Giant Rotation	12
Strange Seasons	13
Green World	15
Patchwork Miranda	16
Wrinkled Ariel	18
Dark Satellite	20
Titania and Oberon	22
Rings of Uranus	23
Voyager's Moonlets	26
Neptune	27
Hunting the Eighth Planet	29
Colourful Atmosphere	33
Watery Generator	39
Battered Moonlets	42
Geysers of Triton	48
Pluto	52
Sorry, Wrong Planet	55
Double Act	57
Cold and Rocky	59
Books to Read	61
Glossary	62
Index	64

Uranus

The last three known planets in the Solar System have an immense stretch of space to themselves and their satellites. The average distance between Saturn and Pluto is about 4,470 million kilometres (2,780 million miles).

Space probes from Earth have now visited all the major planets in the Solar System. Together with their moons and the asteroids, they all orbit the Sun with a precise regularity that is the basis of our own system of time.

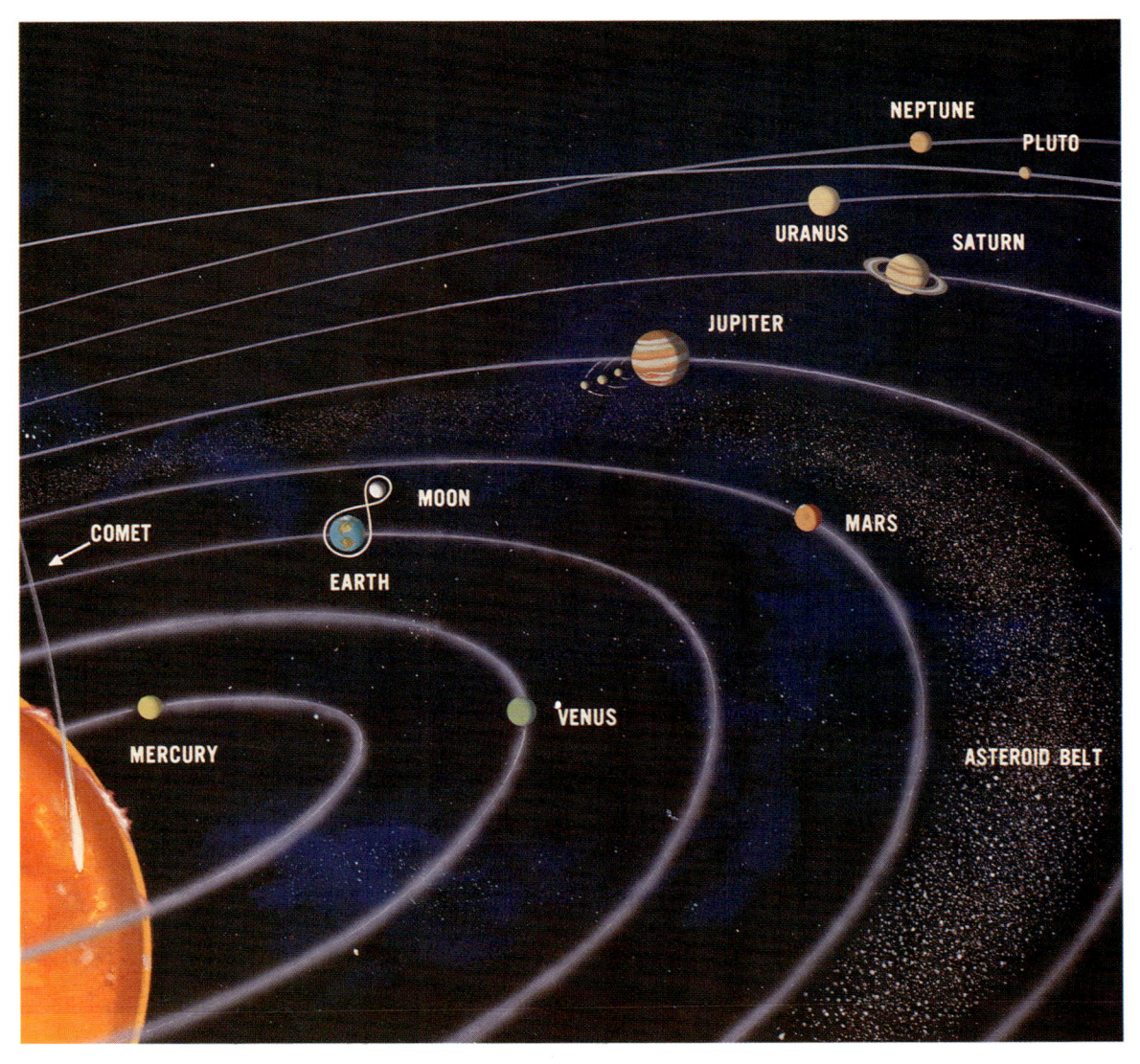

This is more than three times the distance of Saturn from the Sun. In this enormous region, Uranus, Neptune and Pluto pursue their lonely orbits. They are still locked into the gravitational pull of the Sun, but very far from its warmth and light.

Familiar Friends

To the ancient astronomers, Saturn was the farthest planet. Mercury, Venus, Mars, Jupiter and Saturn were all familiar thousands of years ago. Shepherds, priests, scientists, farmers and sailors could follow their paths as they wandered against the background of stars. People in early civilizations could see these planets with the naked eye. Yet even after the telescope had made its appearance, no planets were added to the ancient list for almost two centuries.

Musical Astronomer

William Herschel was a professional musician and an enthusiastic amateur astronomer. He worked in Bath, in the west of England, as a chapel organist and composer. After he read a book about the science of *optics,* Herschel began to teach himself how to make telescopes, especially reflecting telescopes, which use mirrors to focus the light rays. They did not suffer from the same colour distortion as the refracting telescopes used by most professional astronomers at the time. Reflectors proved best for the observation of fine detail, while refractors were better adapted to the task of measuring star positions accurately.

William Herschel made excellent telescopes. His most famous instrument was a large reflecting telescope, completed in 1789. A smaller Herschel reflector is shown below.

Sky Search

Eventually, Herschel was constructing telescopes of better quality than those used at the *Royal*

> ## Uranus Facts
> Average distance from Sun: 2,870,000,000 km (1,783,000,000 miles)
> Nearest distance from Earth: 2,720,000,000 km (1,690,000,000 miles)
> Average temperature (clouds): –140°C (–220°F)
> Diameter across equator: 52,000 km (32,000 miles)
> Atmosphere: Hydrogen, helium
> Number of moons: 15 known
> Length of day: 17¼ hours
> Length of year: 84 Earth years

Greenwich Observatory. He began a systematic search of the skies in 1779, cataloguing *double stars,* pairs of stars that appear to be close together in the sky. He hoped to detect a slight movement, over a period of six months, of one component of a double star with respect to the other. Such a displacement would enable him to calculate the distance from Earth to a star, something no one had achieved at that time.

The Curious Comet

Herschel had built his first telescope in 1774, but on the night of Tuesday 13 March 1781, he was using one of his later instruments a reflector with a 15-centimetre (6-inch) aperture and a focal length of 1·8 metres (6 feet). He had already used it extensively to discover double stars, as well as galaxies beyond the *Milky Way.* That night, according to his log book, Herschel discovered a double star in the constellation of Gemini. One component of the double star was 'a curious either Nebulous Star or perhaps a Comet'.

Herschel was puzzled by his new find because he knew that stars, whatever the magnification of the telescope, should appear as points of twinkling light. What he saw on this occasion, however, was a small disc. He announced the discovery of his new 'comet' to the Bath Philosophical Society and to the prestigious Royal Society in London.

Naming a New Planet

Over a period of several weeks, a number of astronomers plotted the movement of the new object. They calculated that it performed an almost circular orbit of the sun at a distance of almost 3,000,000,000 kilometres (1,860,000,000 miles). There

William Herschel discovered Uranus which he initially thought was a comet. During the weeks following his discovery, it was calculated that the planet had an almost circular orbit of the sun. This confirmed that Herschel had in fact discovered a new planet.

was no doubt about it, William Herschel had discovered a new planet. It was an earth-shattering event in public as well as scientific circles. No one had ever discovered a planet before. Herschel wanted to call his find 'Georgium Sidus' (George's Star) in honour of King George III. Some astronomers insisted on calling the new planet 'Herschel' for a while. However, Herschel's contemporary, Johann Bode, suggested that it was more fitting to carry on the tradition of naming planets after characters from classical Graeco-Roman mythology. He proposed to call the planet 'Uranus', the father of Saturn, just as Saturn had been the father of Jupiter, and Jupiter had been the father of Mars.

Career Change

Herschel was praised and acclaimed throughout the scientific world for his discovery. George III made him a knight and gave him a private observatory near Windsor, along with a pension. So Herschel was able to become a full-time astronomer and telescope maker. He discovered two satellites of Uranus, Titania and Oberon, in 1787. Two years later, he also discovered two satellites of Saturn, Mimas and Enceladus. Herschel continued to improve his telescopes and built the largest telescope in the world, a 122-centimetre (48-inch) reflector, to help in surveying the skies visible in the northern hemisphere. He correctly calculated that our galaxy, the *Milky Way Galaxy*, is a spiral-shaped disc star system, and that our Sun is just one of its component stars. He was also the first to recognize that some of the *nebulae* already discovered out in space were in fact other galaxies like our own.

Old Records

As scientists searched the records of earlier astronomers, it became apparent that Uranus had been noted on a number of occasions in the past. However,

Uranus shows blue-green in this Voyager 2 image, because the small amount of methane gas in the planet's atmosphere absorbs light in the red part of the spectrum.

those seeing it had always recorded it on their charts as a star. There had been at least twenty previous recorded sightings, the earliest in 1690. The information collected from these earlier sightings showed irregularities in Uranus's orbits. This led to the discovery of Neptune.

Voyager 2 took this picture of a crescent-shaped Uranus as it left the planet behind and continued its journey, heading for Neptune. The blue atmosphere of Uranus pales almost to white at the extreme edge of the crescent because of haze around the planet.

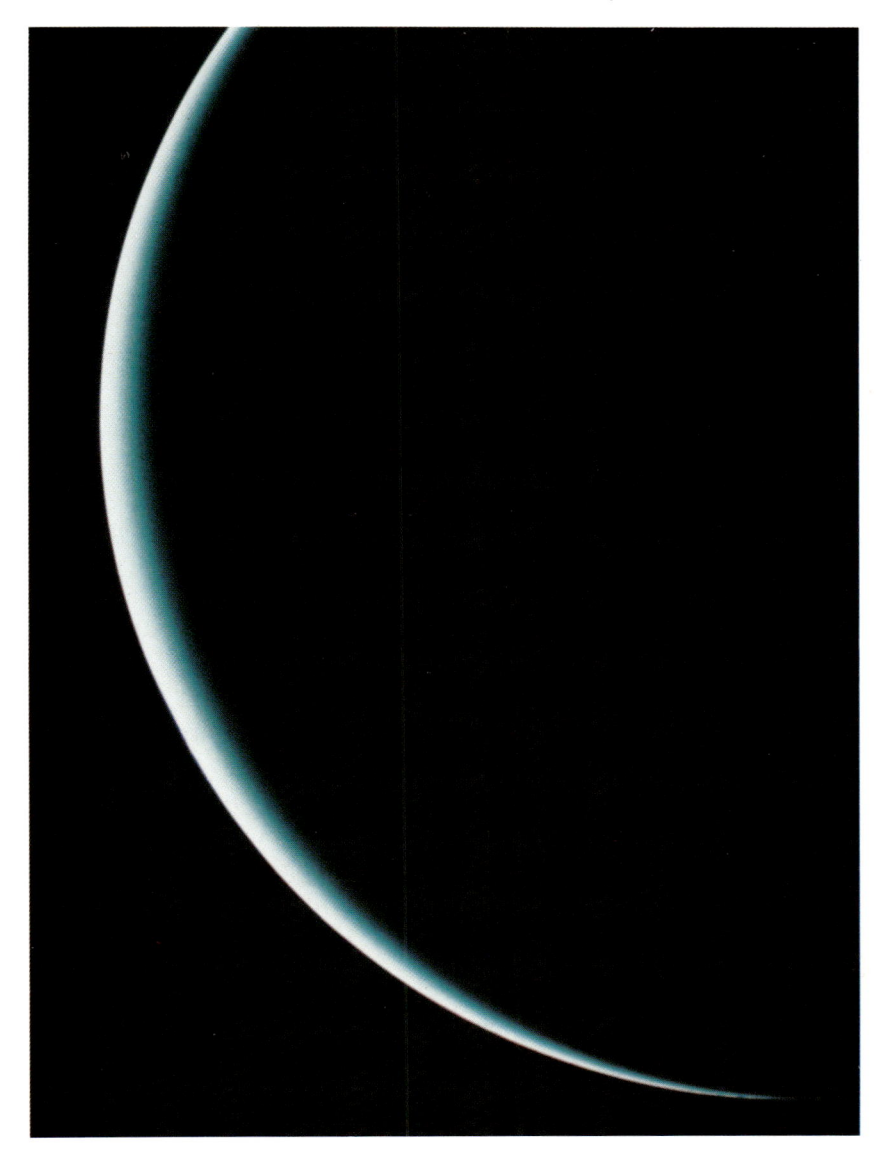

Uranus is an average distance of 2,720,000,000 kilometres (1,690,000,000 miles) from Earth. If we look at Uranus through a telescope, we see a dim, greenish disc with no detailed markings. At such a huge distance, it takes the light, and therefore the images we see, 2 hours 45 minutes to reach Earth.

Gas Giant Rotation

The diameter of Uranus is about 52,000 kilometres (32,000 miles) at its equator, and it rotates on its own axis once every 17¼ hours. Because we can detect no distinguishing features on Uranus from Earth, it was impossible to get an accurate idea of its rate of rotation

Voyager 2 encountered Uranus while the green planet's southern pole was going through a period of unbroken sunlight. The dark rings of Uranus, visible here, were discovered from Earth in 1977. Voyager discovered one previously unknown ring.

> **Did You Know?**
> In 1977, astronomers discovered that Uranus has a set of narrow rings. Scientists think that there are ten rings in all. They are made of the darkest material so far found in the
> Solar System.

until it was surveyed by the space probe Voyager 2 in 1986. Even then, the first cloud images, taken through an orange filter to bring out detail, showed a rate of rotation of about 16 hours. This calculation was a combination of planetary rotation rate and wind speeds. To measure the *deep interior rotation rate*, Voyager had to examine the planet's magnetic field. Scientists studied movements in the planet's magnetotail, the trailing, twisting taper of the planet's magnetosphere, or magnetic field envelope. By timing bursts of radio-wave energy, they established a deep interior rotation rate of 17 hours 14 minutes.

Planet on its Side

The unique characteristic of Uranus among the other planets is the tilt of its axis of rotation, which is at an angle of 98° to the vertical. This means that, instead of spinning in a relatively upright position as it goes round the Sun, it lies on its side.

Strange Seasons

It takes Uranus a stately 84 Earth years to complete one circuit of the Sun. Because of the unusual angle at which it spins, the planet has strange periods of exposure to the Sun's rays. For 42 Earth years, one pole of Uranus receives some degree of sunlight, while the other pole is in darkness. For the next 42 years, their positions are reversed. The equatorial regions, meanwhile, experience two winters and two summers each Uranian year.

Navigator's Nightmare

On Earth, the magnetic poles do not quite coincide with the 'true' poles at each end of the rotational axis. Earth's magnetic axis is inclined to the spin axis by 11·6°. It passes through the planet on a line which misses the centre of the sphere by about 400 kilometres (250 miles). For this reason, Earth-bound navigators have to make slight adjustments to their *compass bearings* to make allowances for the difference between *magnetic north* and true north. Navigators on Uranus would have an almost impossible task. There, the magnetic axis is inclined at 60° to the spin axis. It misses the planet's centre by more than 8,000 kilometres (5,000 miles), and the magneto-tail stretches away from the planet in a twisting, corkscrew path.

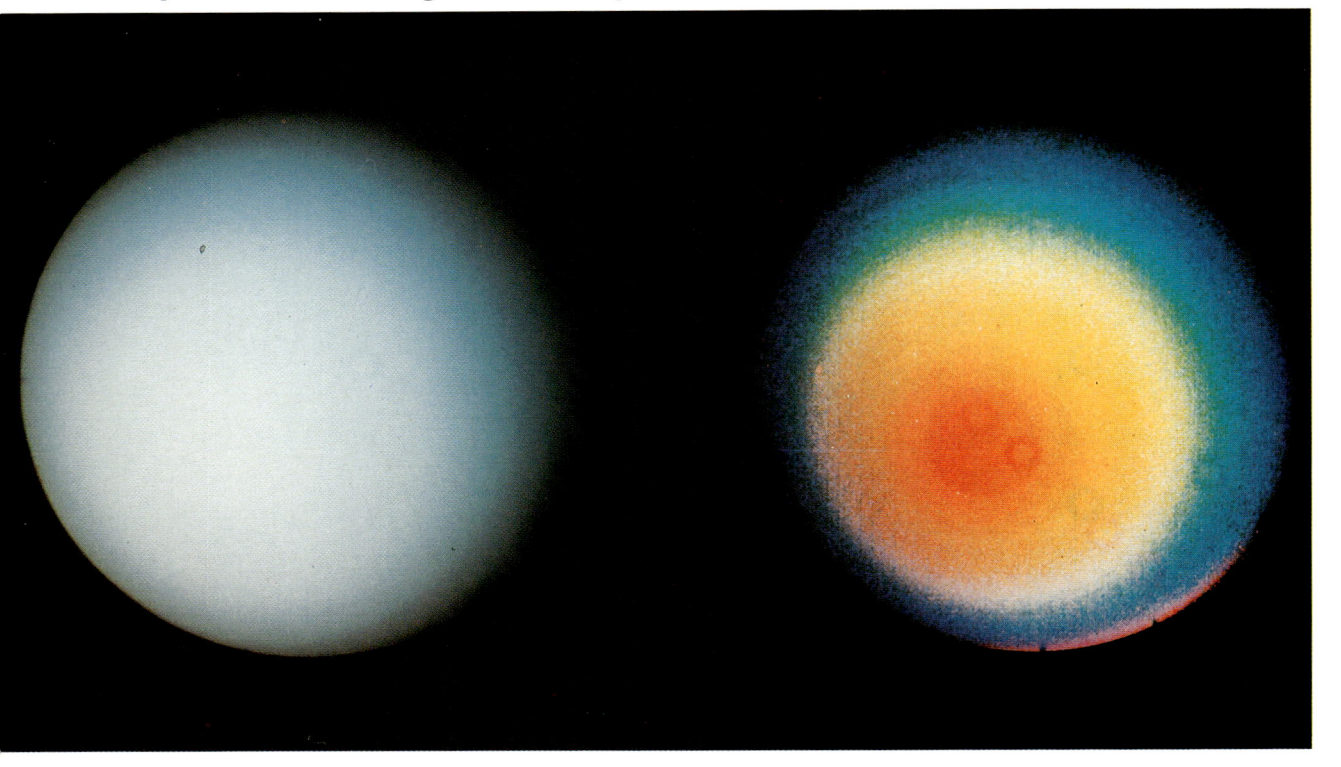

Magnetic Ocean

Uranus has a *density* 1·23 times that of water. Its mass is 14·6 times that of Earth. The planet has a dense core, probably of rock and ice, which is about the size of Earth. That centre is surrounded by a planet-covering 'ocean' of hot water 8,000 kilometres (5,000 miles) deep. The planet's strong magnetic field is somehow generated within this liquid mantle, perhaps by the movement of solid elements in it. Certainly Uranus cannot contain the highly conductive metallic hydrogen that exists on Jupiter and Saturn. That would require pressures and temperatures far higher than anything on Uranus.

When Uranus is seen in true colour *(left)*, it presents us with a smooth, featureless exterior. However, a false-colour image *(right)*, captured with special filters and extreme-contrast computer enhancement, reveals that we are looking directly at the planet's pole, surrounded by bands of cloud or fog.

14

Right: False-colour images also reveal activity in the planet's upper atmosphere. Orange-filter pictures of Uranus have shown the presence of white clouds in the blue atmosphere beyond the polar haze.

Below: A sequence of time-lapse pictures traces the movement of the white clouds over a 4½-hour period, through a combination of the planet's rotation and upper atmospheric winds.

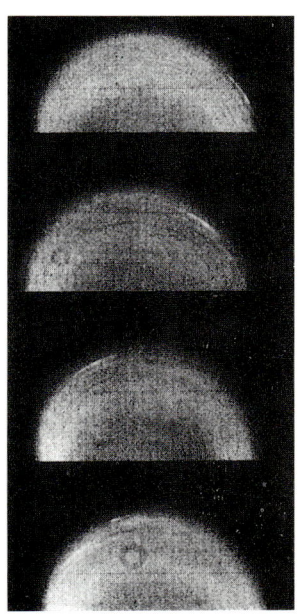

Green World

Above the water layer, Uranus has a thick atmosphere containing about 84 per cent hydrogen, 14 per cent helium, and 2 per cent methane, with traces of acetylene and methane. This atmosphere may be 10,000 kilometres (6,200 miles) deep. We see Uranus as a blue-green disc because the methane in the atmosphere absorbs the red component of sunlight.

Like the other gaseous planets, Uranus does not have a sharply delineated 'surface'. It does have a region where molecules of water vapour, methane and ammonia give way to the helium-rich mixture of the atmosphere itself. At the level in the atmosphere where atmospheric pressure is about 1·3 Earth atmospheres, and the temperature is −193°C (−315°F), there is a layer of clouds formed of methane crystals.

Before the Voyager encounter, there were five known moons of Uranus. William Herschel had discovered two of them, Titania and Oberon, in 1787. Two more, Umbriel and Ariel, were discovered in 1851 by the English astronomer, William Lassell. The fifth, Miranda, was found in 1948 by an American astronomer, Gerard Kuiper.

Patchwork Miranda

Miranda is the innermost moon, orbiting the planet at a distance of 129,400 kilometres (80,400 miles) once every 1·4 days. Like the others, it is dark and icy. It

The southern hemisphere of Miranda, the smallest of the major moons of Uranus. Miranda has a patchy surface, and three distinct areas of the once-fragmented moon are visible.

In this composite image, Voyager 2 skims close to Miranda, coming within 29,000 kilometres (18,000 miles) of the moon.

has a diameter of 480 kilometres (300 miles) and a density 1.3 times that of water. Voyager 2 came within 29,000 kilometres (18,000 miles) of Miranda and sent images back to the *Jet Propulsion Laboratory* showing one of the strangest moons in the Solar System. The surface of Miranda looks like patchwork or a jigsaw puzzle, that has been put together in a hurry. The parts all fit together, but the seams show, and the surface patterns of the segments show terrains that bear little or no relation to one another.

Reassembled Moon

Some regions of Miranda show evidence of dramatic geological activity, with steep valleys and cliffs sculpted in the moon's crust by internal stresses. There are some *impact craters* with smooth, ancient profiles, and others with crisp, far more recent outlines. Cliffs and scarps between 10 and 15 kilometres (6 and 10 miles) high seem out of all proportion to the diminutive size of Miranda. The logical explanation for the strange, abruptly juxtaposed terrains that make up Miranda's surface is that at some time in the past this moon was smashed into fragments by a large meteorite. Instead of floating off to form smaller satellites, the pieces stayed close enough to each other to be brought back together

17

by gravitational attraction. Eventually, they regrouped into a sizeable moon. The heat caused by the regrouping would have resulted in some melting and remoulding, but evidence of the re-assembly would still show, as in the jumbled terrains we see today.

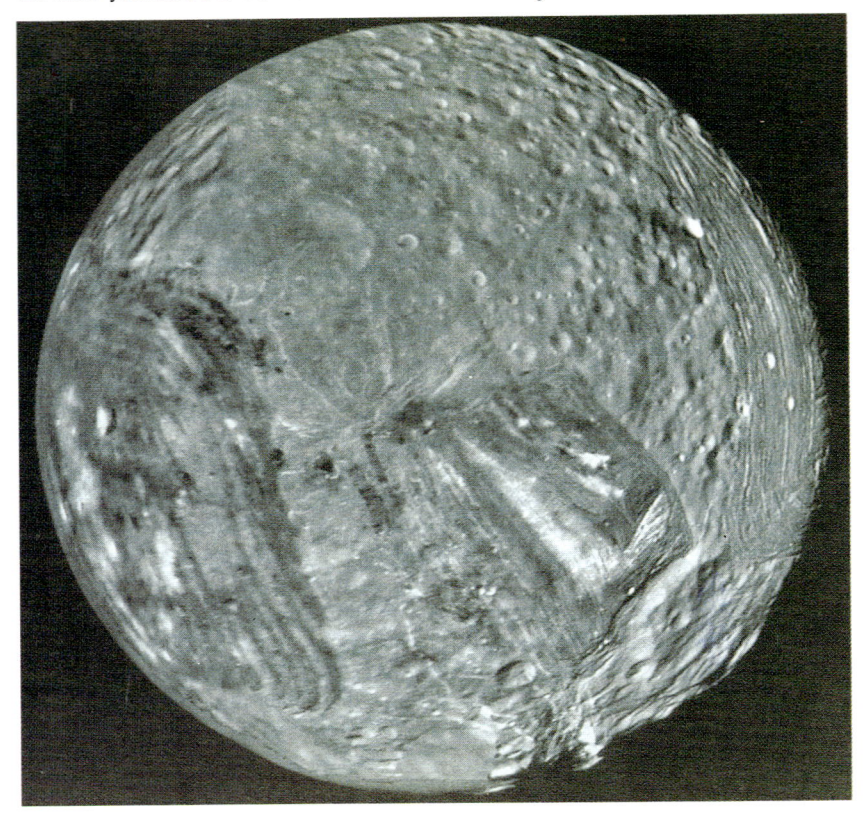

Miranda reveals its southern polar view in this mosaic of nine separate photographs. Voyager achieved extremely sharp pictures of Miranda, with a resolution down to 600 metres (2,000 feet). Miranda's surface is a jumble of regions of valleys, cliffs and craters.

Wrinkled Ariel

Farther out from Miranda, 191,000 kilometres (118,700 miles) from Uranus, the moon Ariel, with a diameter of 1,160 kilometres (720 miles), orbits the planet once every 2½ days. Voyager took clear pictures of Ariel, showing it to have a mixture of old and new impact craters, and evidence of an active geological past. The

> ### Did You Know?
> The Roman God Uranus was the father of Saturn, who deposed him, and the grandfather of Jupiter.

At a junction of different surface regions, Miranda displays deep ice-cliffs, close-packed valleys and an overlay of crisply defined meteorite craters.

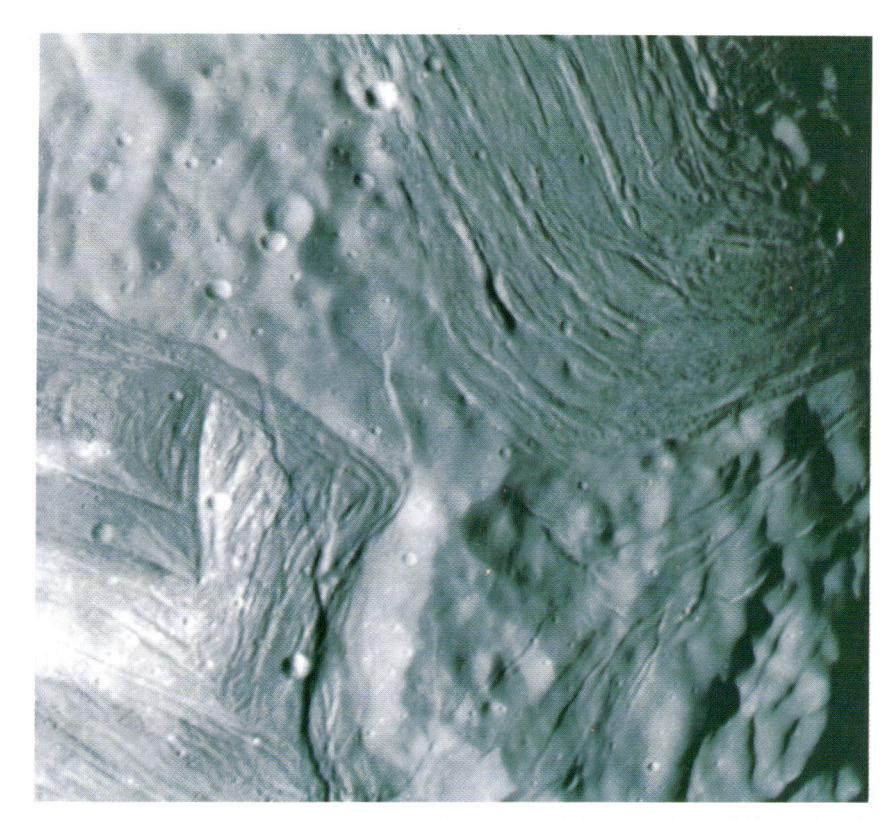

The well-cratered surface of Ariel is deeply scarred with fault features, such as the scarps and valleys visible here. The bottoms of the largest of these valleys contain deposits from a more recent period.

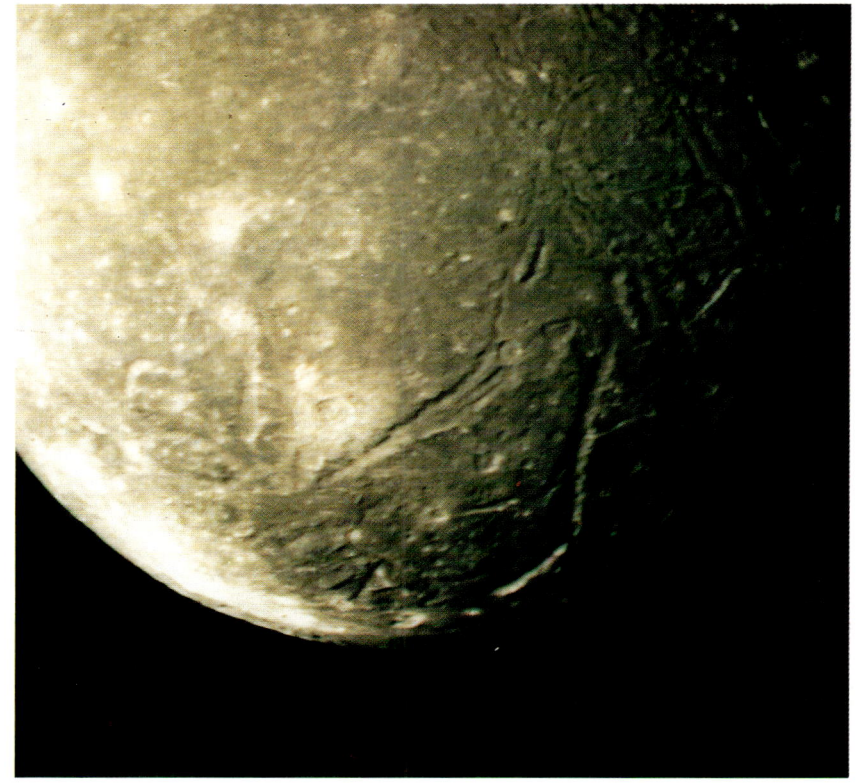

crust has stretched and cracked into valleys. Some of them are deep and have broad floors which have been flooded at some point with flows of ice or molten material.

Dark Satellite

Umbriel, the next moon out from Uranus, is very dark and ancient. It has a diameter of 1,190 kilometres (740 miles) and an orbit 266,000 kilometres (165,000 miles) from the planet, which it completes once every 4·14 days. Umbriel's surface, which reflects only 16 per cent of the dim sunlight reaching it, is pocked with old

Umbriel is the darkest of the moons of Uranus, named after the 'dark angel' in Alexander Pope's poem, *The Rape of the Lock*. The bright ring near the moon's visible edge is about 30 kilometres (20 miles) in diameter. Scientists have so far been unable to explain this bright feature on an otherwise gloomy moon, which is heavily pocked with impact craters. All the satellites of Uranus have surfaces of dirty ice, but Umbriel may have received a denser fall of dark debris than the others.

craters, some of which are 200 kilometres (125 miles) in diameter. Umbriel is so much darker than the other large moons that scientists think it may be covered with a dark dust layer. In just one region of the moon, the Voyager cameras picked out a bright, doughnut-shaped ring. It could be internal material such as ice which has been splashed out on to the surface by a meteorite impact, or may have been forced out by some geological process.

Titania is the largest of Uranus's satellites. The surface is covered with pulverized rock.

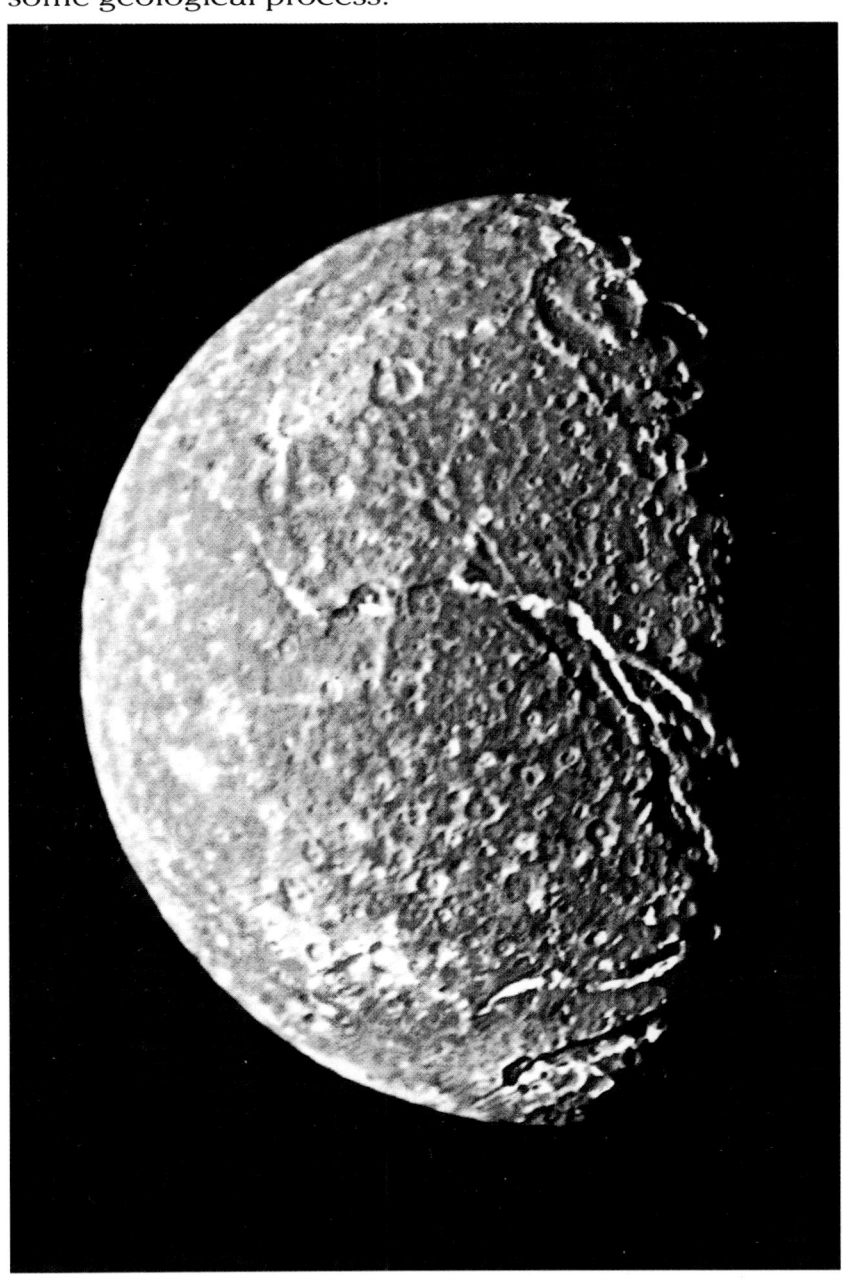

Titania and Oberon

Titania is the fourth of the moons of Uranus visible from Earth. It is also the largest, with a diameter of 1,590 kilometres (988 miles). Titania and Ariel both have a density 1·6 times that of water, revealing that they have a high proportion of rock in their make-up. Enormous valleys 1,600 kilometres (1,000 miles) long and up to 80 kilometres (50 miles) wide are probably the result of internal ice expansion cracking the surface. They wind across the moon's surface between regions thick with old, eroded craters, some of them 400 kilometres (250 miles) across. Titania orbits Uranus once every 8·71 days at a distance of 435,900 kilometres (270,900 miles).

Titania was discovered by William Herschel in 1787, at the same time that he discovered Oberon. The cratered surface, with its long fault valleys, shows that Titania has suffered considerable geological upheaval.

Oberon, the outermost moon, is the only one with impact craters surrounded by bright rays, which may be clean ice that has been splashed out. Inside some of the craters are dark patches of material which may have welled up mixed with water in some early volcanic activity. Oberon is slightly smaller than Titania, with a diameter of just under 1,550 kilometres (960 miles). It orbits Uranus at a distance of 583,300 kilometres (362,500 miles) once every 13½ Earth days.

The Voyager flights were more ambitious than those of any previous space probes. Voyager 1 (blue track) made close passes of Jupiter and Saturn, while Voyager 2 (red track) went on to explore the systems of Uranus and Neptune.

Rings of Uranus

In 1977, the year the Voyager probes began their mammoth journeys across the Solar System, astronomers on Earth made a momentous discovery about Uranus. They knew that, in March, Uranus was due to pass in front of a star in the Libra constellation – to *occult* it. Teams of observers prepared to watch, for when a planet occults a star, astronomers can learn a lot about its atmosphere, size and position. They study changes

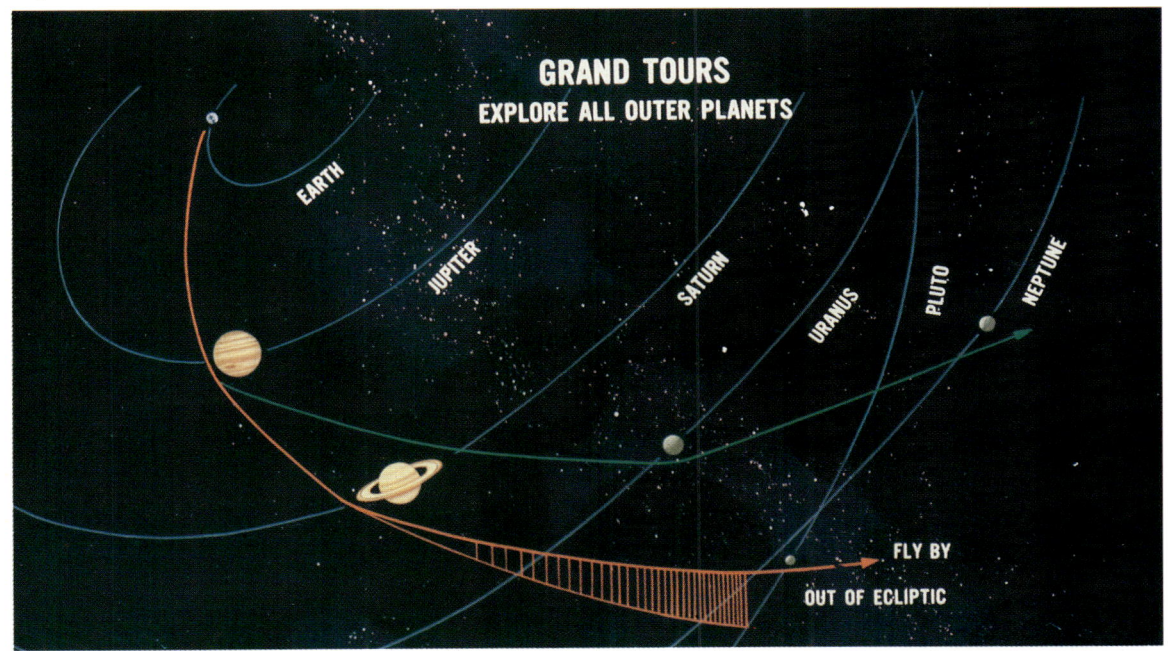

This Voyager image of Oberon shows its ray craters, created by the outward splashing of bright material, such as ice, during a meteorite impact. The central crater in this image contains dark material which may have erupted into the crater after its formation. The protruding mountain peak at the moon's lower-left horizon is 6 kilometres (4 miles) high.

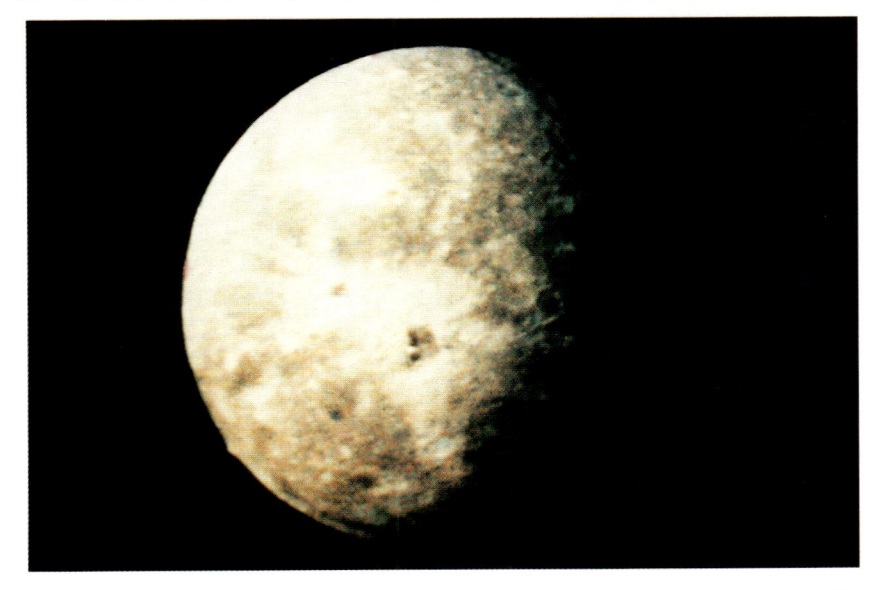

> ### Did You Know?
> One of the strangest things about Uranus is that it 'rolls' round the Sun. All the other planets spin like tops. On Uranus, either the northern or southern hemisphere faces the Sun. It receives sunlight, while the other hemisphere remains in almost total darkness. This creates the Solar System's longest seasons, with summer and winter each lasting about 21 years.

in the star's light emission when it is close to the edge of the planet.

In the 40 minutes before and after the star was

The rings of Uranus, shown in this artist's impression, were first discovered by NASA's Kuiper Airborne Observatory in 1977. Although the rings are bright in this picture, they are actually extremely dark and narrow, reflecting almost no light.

In these computer-constructed slices of the Epsilon rings of Uranus, the redder areas contain less orbiting material. The smaller slice is 22 kilometres (14 miles) across, and the larger is 32 kilometres (20 miles) across, for the rings appear to change width as they circle the planet, becoming widest at the farthest distance.

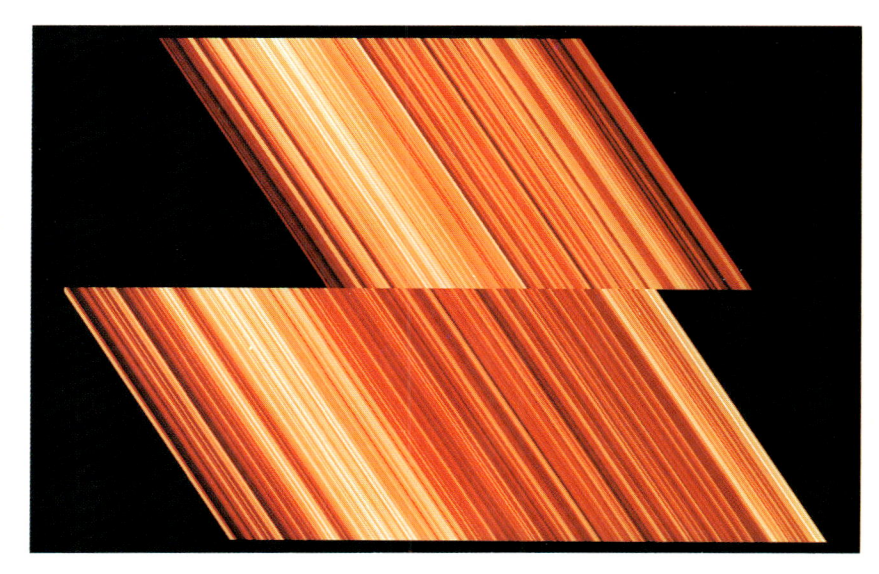

masked by the planet, the observers were surprised to see the star's light dim several times. The dimmings were symmetrical — the same number occurred before the *occultation* as after it. The only explanation was that Uranus has a system of rings, like Saturn's but narrower and less extensive.

Further occultations that year and the following year allowed astronomers to establish the presence of nine distinct rings. The Voyager 2 probe confirmed them and found a tenth ring. The Uranian rings are dark, and the material that forms them is probably carbonaceous. They range in width from about 1·6 kilometres (1 mile) to 90 kilometres (55 miles), and they stay in position round the planet's equator in a band between 41,850 kilometres (26,000 miles) and 51,160 kilometres (31,800 miles) from the planet. The effects of the rings on radio signals indicate that the particles in the rings are larger than those in the Saturn ring system. In at least one ring, there were very few particles smaller than 1 metre (3 feet) across.

Epsilon Enigma

The rings of Uranus are very thin, with a thickness of no more than a few metres. The outer ring, known as the Epsilon ring, is much wider than the others, and is slightly eccentric. On one side, it is 800 kilometres (500 miles) wide; on the opposite side, where it is farthest from Uranus, the Epsilon ring is almost 100 kilometres (62 miles) wide.

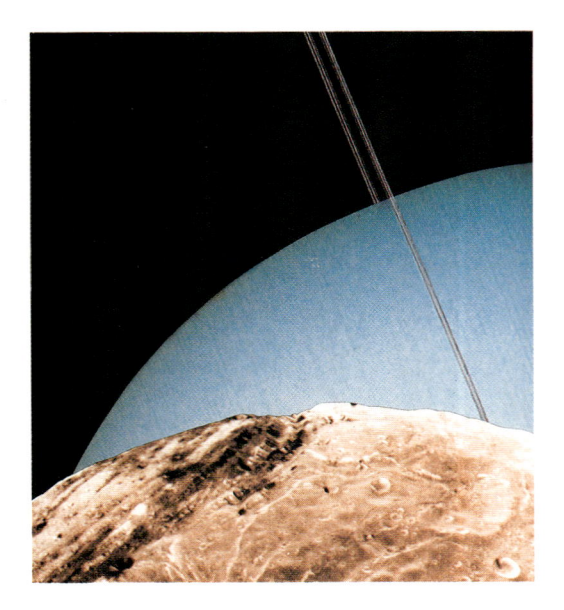

The moon Miranda is in the foreground of this artist's impression, with the blue sphere of Uranus beyond it, encircled by the dark, slender line of the rings.

Voyager's Moonlets

Having noticed the way in which *Shepherd moons* keep the particles of some of Saturn's rings in place, the Voyager team were on the look-out for the same thing with Uranus. Ten small moons were discovered on the Voyager images, though they included only one pair of shepherd moons. These two, named Cordelia and Ophelia, straddle the orbit of the Epsilon ring, 2,000 kilometres (1,250 miles) on each side of it. All the moons discovered by Voyager are small and dark, and, with the exception of Cordelia, they orbit the planet between the outer edge of the Epsilon ring and the orbit of Miranda.

Diameters and Orbiting Distances of Uranus's Small Moons

Moon	Diameter in Kilometres (miles)	Orbiting Distance in Kilometres (miles)
Cordelia	15 (9$\frac{1}{3}$)	49,300 (30,600)
Ophelia	20 (12½)	53,300 (33,120)
Bianca	50 (30)	59,100 (36,725)
Cressida	70 (45)	61,800 (38,400)
Desdemona	50 (30)	62,700 (39,000)
Juliet	70 (45)	64,400 (40,000)
Portia	90 (55)	66,100 (41,000)
Rosalind	50 (30)	69,900 (43,435)
Belinda	50 (30)	75,100 (46,700)
Puck	170 (105)	85,900 (53,400)

Neptune

The orbit of Uranus is not perfectly circular. It has an eccentricity of 0·046. At *perihelion,* it is 2,742,000,000 kilometres (1,704,000,000 miles) from the Sun. At *aphelion,* the distance is 3,008,000,000 kilometres (1,870,000,000 miles). After William Herschel had discovered Uranus, its orbit was very carefully plotted by astronomers. They painstakingly measured the planet's steady movement across the sky relative to the starry background. They were able to establish that Uranus's orbit was elliptical, although, of course, no one could observe complete orbits, since the orbital period of Uranus is a few days over 84 years.

Hidden Influence

The scientists knew that there would be various wobbles and fluctuations in the planet's orbit because of the gravitational influence of other planets. In those days, before computers, it was a mammoth task to figure out all these effects. The work was helped a little by the old astronomical records noting the 'star' that turned out to be Uranus, but the planet did not seem to be behaving in quite the way that scientists had expected. Several astronomers became convinced that

Neptune Facts

Average distance from Sun: 4,500,000,000 km (2,800,000,000 miles)
Nearest distance from Earth: 4,350,000,000 km (2,700,000,000 miles)
Average temperature (clouds): −210°C (−350°F)
Diameter across equator: 48,600 km (30,200 miles)
Atmosphere: Hydrogen, helium, methane
Number of moons: 2 + 6 moonlets
Length of day: 16 hours 3 minutes
Length of year: 165 Earth years

an unknown planet, beyond the orbit of Uranus, was exerting an influence on it.

Unpredictable Wanderer

In the 1820s, a French astronomer-mathematician, Alexis Bouvard, produced tables that could be used to predict the motions of Jupiter, Saturn and Uranus. The calculations proved accurate for Jupiter and Saturn,

In 1845 John Couch Adams, calculated the position where Neptune should be looked for. Unfortunately his calculations were not followed up immediately. In 1846, Johann Galle and Heinrich d'Arrest, working with similar figures calculated by the French astronomer Urbain Leverrier, discovered the planet from the Berlin Observatory.

which moved in exactly the way predicted by the tables. Uranus, however, moved increasingly away from its predicted path.

Hunting the Eighth Planet

Two scientists, working independently, eventually worked their way through the mass of longhand calculations needed to pinpoint the reason for Uranus's disturbed orbit. In England, John Couch Adams, a mathematician at Cambridge University, was sure, in September 1845, that he knew where to look for the 'eighth planet'. He also predicted the mass and orbit of the mystery planet. His calculations had taken him two years. Unfortunately, the Astronomer Royal at Greenwich Observatory, George Airy, failed to respond immediately to the calculations, and almost nothing was done in England to find the new planet.

Meanwhile, in France, the astronomer Urbain Leverrier was coming to almost identical conclusions to Adams. Leverrier published his results in June 1846, and these at last prompted a search for the new planet.

A search began in England on 29 July 1846. The Director of Cambridge University Observatory, James

Uranus and Neptune are huge compared to our own planet Earth, with diameters of 50,800 kilometres (31,567 miles) and 48,600 kilometres (30,200 miles) respectively, against Earth's 12,757 kilometres (7,927 miles).

Challis, started a systematic survey using the 30-cm (11¾-inch) Northumberland refracting telescope at the observatory. Challis actually saw the new planet twice, but thought it was a star.

Neptune Surfaces

On 23 September 1846, Johann Galle and Heinrich d'Arrest, using Leverrier's calculations, searched the relevant area of the sky from the Berlin Observatory in Germany and found the new planet. The following night, the German astronomers checked their new find and were gratified to see that it had moved relative to the stars around it. The Berlin astronomers called the new planet 'Neptune', after the god of the sea in classical mythology.

Moon Family

Less than a month after Galle and d'Arrest found Neptune, an English astronomer, William Lassell, discovered its moon, Triton. Over a century later, in May 1949, the American astronomer, Gerard Kuiper, discovered another satellite of Neptune, called Nereid.

Urbain Leverrier worked out the position of the planet Neptune at the same time as John Couch Adams. Neither was aware of the other's work on the subject.

> **Did You Know?**
> Neptune was the first planet to be discovered by mathematical calculations instead of by eye. However, it had been registered as a star in 1795 by a French astronomer named Lalande.

When the Voyager 2 probe reached Neptune in August 1989, it sent back images of six small, previously unknown satellites, ranging from 30 to 300 kilometres (20 to 200 miles) in diameter.

This is a full-scale Voyager model, used at the Jet Propulsion Laboratory during the Neptune approach so that new procedures could be pre-tested. On the right is the imaging apparatus; on the left, the radioisotope thermoelectric generator.

Neptune has an equatorial diameter of 48,600 kilometres (30,200 miles). It is slightly smaller than Uranus, though it has a larger mass — 17·23 times the mass of Earth — and a density 1·64 times that of water. Neptune orbits the Sun at an average distance of 4,500,000,000 kilometres (2,800,000,000 miles), and it takes it 165 years to complete one orbit. Neptune has not completed one orbit of the Sun since it was identified.

Voyager 2 photographed a new satellite of Neptune, N1, on 25 August 1989, from a distance of 146,500 kilometres (91,000 miles). N1 is irregular in shape, with an average radius of 200 kilometres (125 miles).

Neptune's 'day' is 16 hours 3 minutes long. Voyager was able to establish the planet's rotational period by timing bursts of radio noise from the planet's magnetic field. Unlike Uranus, which rotates 'on its back' at an angle of 98° to the vertical, Neptune sits relatively upright as it spins, with its rotational axis at an angle of about 29°.

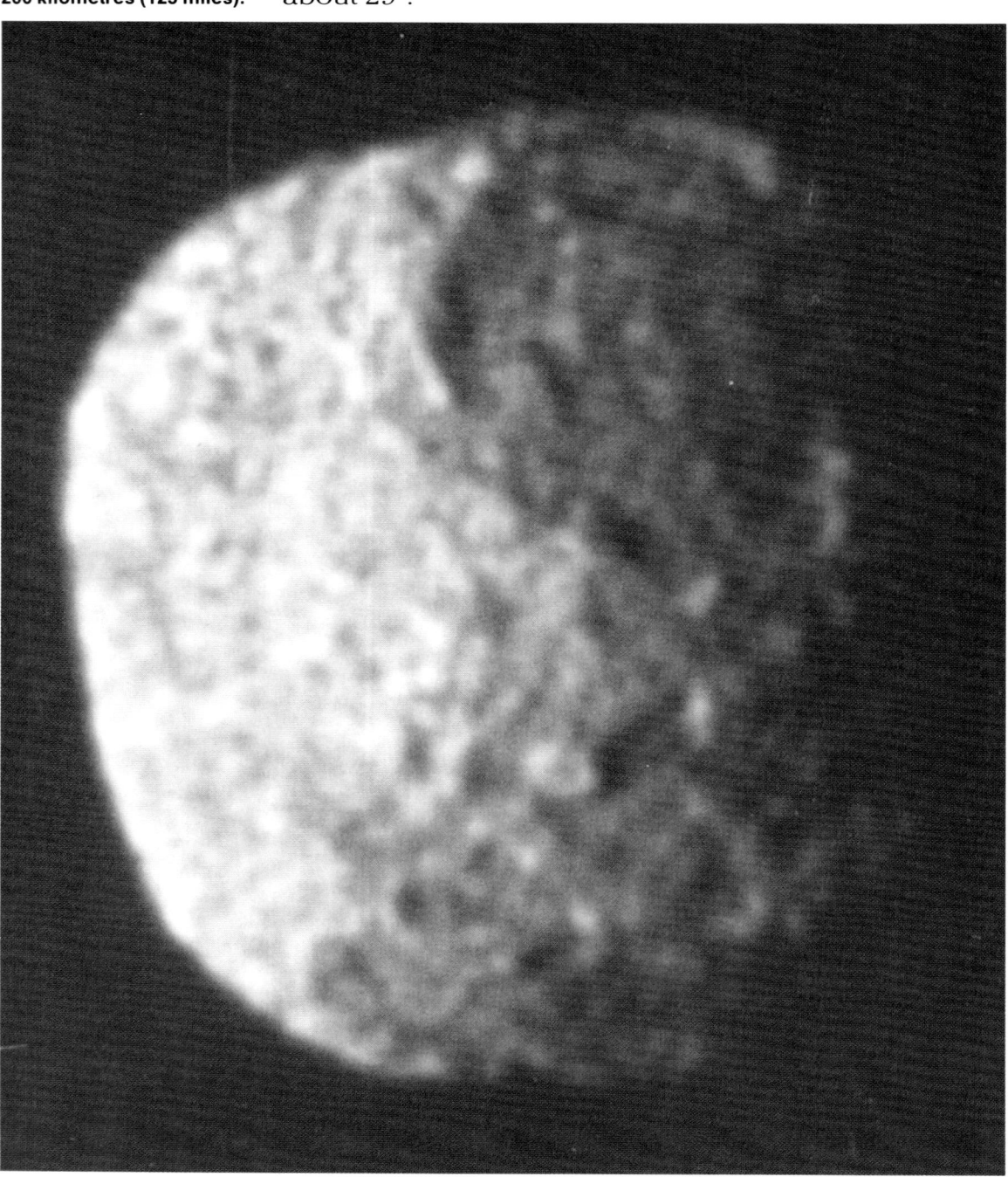

The bright red rim of Neptune in this colour-filtered image reveals the planet's outer haze. This scatters the rays of the Sun before they reach the methane in the atmosphere. Unaffected by the strong methane spectrum, red light shines round the planet, while at deeper atmospheric levels the methane effectively cancels out red light, leaving Neptune's main disc bright blue. The white markings are areas of cloud which are also high enough to remain unaffected by atmospheric methane's light-absorbing qualities.

Colourful Atmosphere

The Neptune revealed by Voyager 2's images was a brilliant blue globe marked with deeper blue features and streaks of white cloud. Voyager discovered a world with a *dynamic atmosphere,* where storm systems the size of Earth are blown around the planet at 1,125 km/h (700 mph). Frozen methane forms white, wispy clouds that stretch in ranks thousands of miles long and cast shadows on the dense blue cloud cover 50 kilometres (30 miles) below.

Unlike Uranus, which gets all the thermal energy that powers its climate from the Sun, Neptune has an internal heat source. At its huge distance from the Sun, solar energy is only a thousandth of what we receive here on Earth. Neptune is dark and cold, but heat from within hurls frozen gases pluming up from the cloud layers. The planet's internal heat also fuels the winds that tear round Neptune and the great whirlwinds which are Neptune's equivalent of Jupiter's great storm spots.

Planetary Peep-hole

Largest of Neptune's storm features is the Great Dark Spot (GDS). The size of Earth, it rotates counter-clockwise once every ten Earth days. The GDS is a deep *vortex* that bores straight through the methane cloud

Like Jupiter, Neptune has a large, seemingly permanent storm region, called the Great Dark Spot. The white streaks visible here are cirrus clouds that usually appear at the Great Dark Spot's boundary, frequently changing their shape and position.

34

layer, which is the blue sphere we see when we look at the planet. The darkness of the GDS is the darkness of the depths of Neptune's atmosphere. It is a rare spy-hole which affords us a look deeper into the atmosphere. The GDS is a high-pressure area. Methane blown over the doming top of the GDS condenses, and gleaming methane ice crystals form long, narrow *cirrus clouds*. They become strung out halfway round the

This close-up of Neptune's cirrus clouds shows them casting their shadows on to the main cloud cover beneath them. These high-altitude bands of cloud are up to 200 kilometres (125 miles) wide.

planet as the GDS steams westwards in the arms of its gale, leaving the clouds in its wake.

Eventually, high in the planet's *stratosphere,* the weak sunlight breaks the methane molecules down and then rearranges them. Transformed into heavier molecules,

Three pictures, taken over a 36-hour period, show that the Great Dark Spot, which is the size of Earth, changes shape constantly. The white clouds surrounding the spot are diverted upwards from lower in the atmosphere.

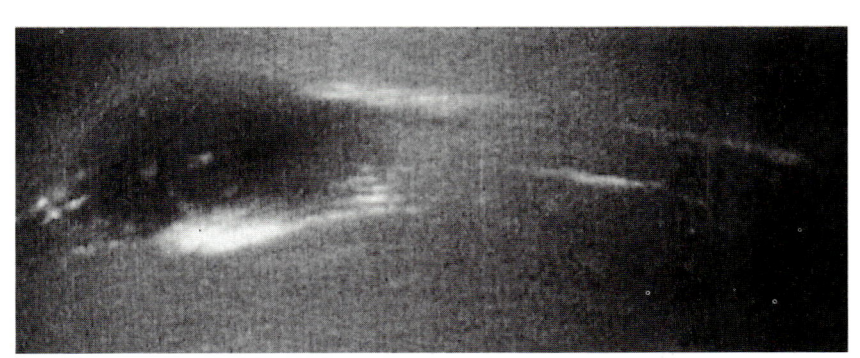

Did You Know?
Neptune has not completed a single orbit of the Sun since it was identified in 1846. Each orbit takes 165 years; at a speed of about 5 kilometres per second (3 miles per second) it will complete its first full orbit in AD 2011.

Stretched into parallel streamers by gales that can reach 2,000 kilometres (1,250 miles) an hour, Neptune's cirrus clouds of methane ice crystals are echoed by dark blue shadows on the thicker cloud cover below.

such as acetylene, they are pulled by gravity as they condense and drop back down to the lower atmosphere.

Cloud Layers

Like Uranus, Neptune has an atmosphere made up mainly of hydrogen, with about 15 per cent helium, a significant 2 per cent or so of methane, and trace elements, such as acetylene and ethane. Closer to the planet than the methane cloud layer we can see, there is another layer, made of hydrogen sulphide. Sometimes this, too, sends plumes up through holes in the methane layer and into the stratosphere.

A white spot, christened 'Scooter' by the Voyager

Did You Know?
The great Italian astronomer, Galileo Galilei, may have been the first scientist to see Neptune. In December 1612, 233 years before its official discovery as a planet, Galileo drew a sketch of a heavenly body close to Jupiter which is likely to have been Neptune.

team, may well be a plume from this deeper layer. Scooter rotates at the same speed as the planet's deep levels. The GDS, on the other hand, takes a couple of hours longer to complete one rotation because it is being carried at considerable speed in the opposite direction to the planet's rotation.

Poles Apart

When scientists at the Jet Propulsion Laboratory first received information from Voyager about Uranus's magnetic field, they were particularly puzzled by the alignment of the magnetic axis. It is at an angle of 60° to the spin axis and misses the planet's centre by more than 8,000 kilometres (5,000 miles). Some thought that this could be due to the unique angle of Uranus's spin axis as it orbits the Sun. Others thought that they had happened upon a planet which was in the middle of reversing its

These two images of Neptune were obtained by Voyager 2. On the left is the planet as it appears without technical enhancement. On the right it is enhanced with the aid of colour filters, and shows the Great Dark Spot in sharp definition.

magnetic field. We know that Earth's magnetic field has reversed in direction every few hundred thousand years. However, when Voyager examined Neptune's magnetic field, it revealed that Neptune's magnetic axis, too, was at an angle of about 50° to its spin axis, and that the magnetic axis missed Neptune's centre by some 10,000 kilometres (6,200 miles).

Watery Generator

It is most unlikely that the two planets would have been reversing their magnetic fields at the same time. Another possibility was that the magnetic fields of

Since its launch in 1977, Voyager 2 has been controlled, and its transmissions decoded, by a dedicated team of experts at Mission Control at the Jet Propulsion Laboratory in Pasadena, California.

Voyager's cameras looked back towards the Sun to take this pair of images in which the Sun's light highlights the dark material which makes up Neptune's thin ring system.

> **Did You Know?**
> Neptune's average distance from the Sun is 4,500 million kilometres (2,800 million miles). This is 30 times the distance between the Earth and the Sun.

Uranus and Neptune are caused in the same way as the skewed magnetic fields of certain stars known as 'oblique rotators'. These stars are thought to have magnetic fields created by the movement of conducting material in their outer layers, not in a metallic core as in Earth. Scientists think that both Uranus and Neptune have non-conducting cores of rock and ice. The most common theory for their magnetic fields is that they are created by the movement of impurities in their watery outer layers

Completing the Circle

As Voyager came close to Neptune, it was able to clear up a problem that had existed since 1984. That year, astronomers had discovered what seemed to be incomplete rings round Neptune. They were arcs of an unidentified material with large gaps in between. Voyager's imagers picked up faint segments joining the arcs, which formed a full, if irregular, outer ring round

> **PIXELS**
> 'Pixel' stands for 'picture element'. A spacecraft's imaging systems are similar to TV cameras. The picture they produce is composed of up to a million dots, or pixels. The on-board computer classifies each pixel according to how light or dark it is. Each pixel's light quality is expressed as a series of two-figure numbers called binary digits. A whole picture of a million pixels could consist of 10 million binary digits. These numbers are transmitted to Earth, where another computer translates them once more into pixels of varying light and shade, to reproduce the original picture.

the planet. The three bright arcs of the outer ring contain much more material than the rest of the ring. When they are viewed from certain angles, they shine, which shows that they are formed of tiny dust particles.

Inside the outer ring, and 10,000 kilometres (6,200 miles) closer to the planet, is another ring. Both the outer rings are very narrow, probably less than 20 kilometres (12½ miles) wide. A third ring, nicknamed 'Fuzzy', is another 10,000 kilometres (6,200 miles) closer to Neptune, and is very broad and diffuse. All three of these rings are in the planet's equatorial plane, as is a fourth ring-like phenomenon.

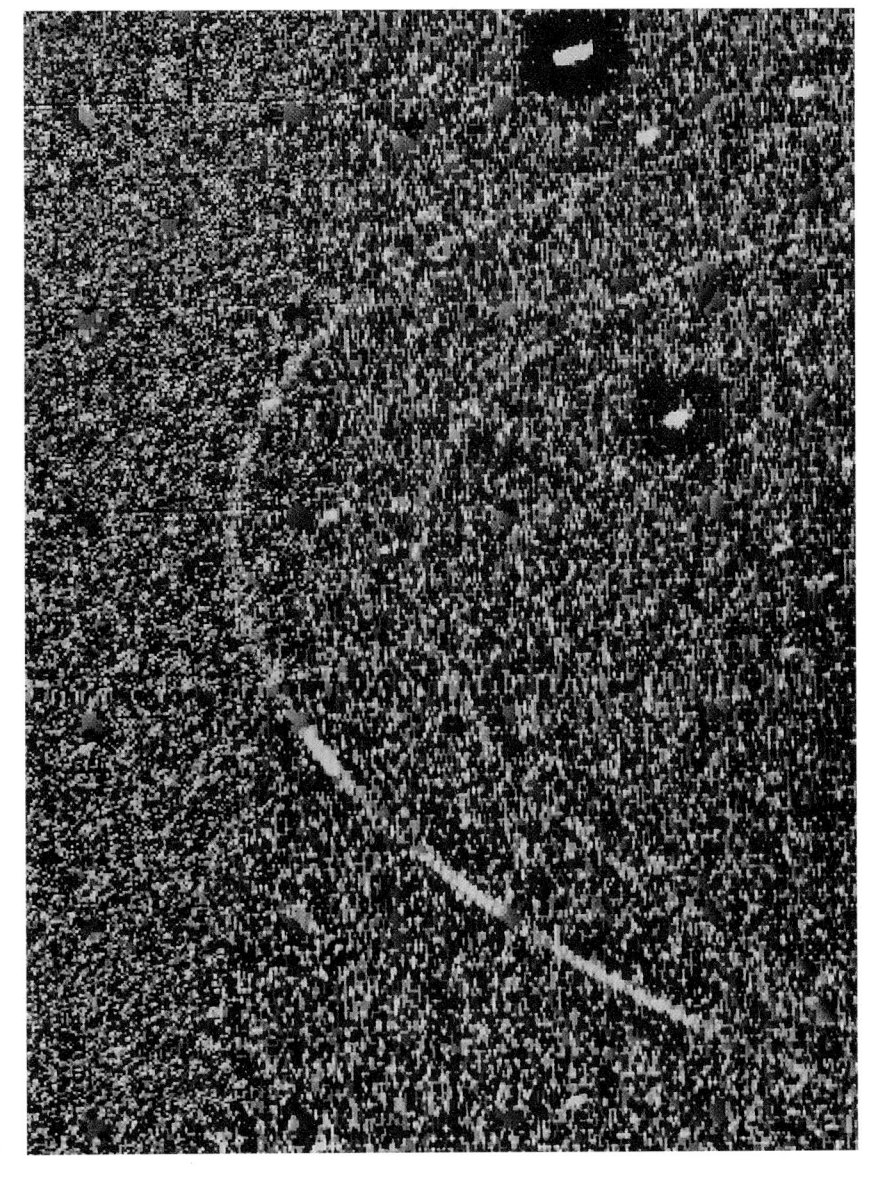

Neptune's outermost ring, 63,000 kilometres (39,000 miles) from the planet, appears to be broken up into a series of short arcs along part of its length. These are areas where ring material clumps together, perhaps due to the gravitational effects of Neptune's moons, one of which can be seen towards the top of the picture which is a pixel image.

> ### Did You Know?
> Uranus and Neptune, like Jupiter and Saturn, have atmospheres that contain helium and hydrogen. However, the atmospheres of Uranus and Neptune also contain methane gas, which makes them look green from Earth.

While Voyager 2 was carrying out its encounter with Neptune, scientists from the USSR joined with those from the United States to work together at the Jet Propulsion Laboratory, sharing this unique moment in the history of space exploration.

This is not so much a ring as a circular sheet of dust, extending from about halfway between the two outer rings all the way down to Neptune's cloud tops.

Battered Moonlets

The six small satellites discovered by Voyager all orbit Neptune in its equatorial plane. All are dark and irregular, because they are too small to have enough gravity to pull them into spherical shape. They all show signs of having been battered by meteorite collisions, and there is no evidence of any melting. They orbit Neptune in the direction of its rotation. The closest one to the planet, 1989 N6, has an orbit 48,200 kilometres (30,000 miles) from the planet, while the farthest, 1989 N1 (which is also the largest), orbits at a distance of 117,600 kilometres (73,000 miles).

Nereid, the moon which was discovered in 1949, is hardly any bigger than the largest of these six new moons, but it orbits Neptune at a huge distance once every 360 Earth days. Its orbit is at a considerable angle to the planet's equatorial plane – about 30° – which indicates that it may have been 'captured' by Neptune.

Orbits in Reverse

Triton, with an orbit at an angle of 20° to Neptune's equatorial plane, has the distinction of being the only moon in the Solar System that orbits its parent planet in a retrograde direction – opposite to the direction of the planet's own rotation.

Bright Reflector

Triton was almost completely unknown before the Voyager encounter. Astronomers knew only that it was there and that it was quite large. Voyager revealed that Triton is smaller than our own Moon, with a diameter of 2,720 kilometres (1,690 miles). Unlike our Moon, however, Triton is highly reflective of the light that

Voyager 2 looks back at Neptune and Triton, one of its two major moons, in this artist's impression. The space probe came within 4,800 kilometres (3,000 miles) of Neptune's cloud tops before carrying out a close fly-by of Triton.

reaches it. A pinkish southern polar cap gives back 80 per cent of incoming light, while the darker northern hemisphere, reddish-brown in tone, reflects 60 per cent of the sunlight reaching it.

Supercold Satellite

Because of its astonishingly high reflectivity, Triton is intensely cold, at $-236°C$ or $(-393°F)$. That makes it the coldest known object in the Solar System. It is also one of only three moons in the Solar System that have an atmosphere. The other two are Jupiter's Io and Saturn's Titan. Triton's atmosphere is mainly nitrogen. Frozen nitrogen and methane form the pink 'snow' over the great southern polar cap of the moon, and near its equator nitrogen and methane snow falls.

At a distance of 350,000 kilometres (220,000 miles) from Neptune, Triton orbits the planet in a retrograde direction, opposite to the planet's own direction of rotation. Alone of the moons of the outer planets, Triton has a well-developed atmosphere.

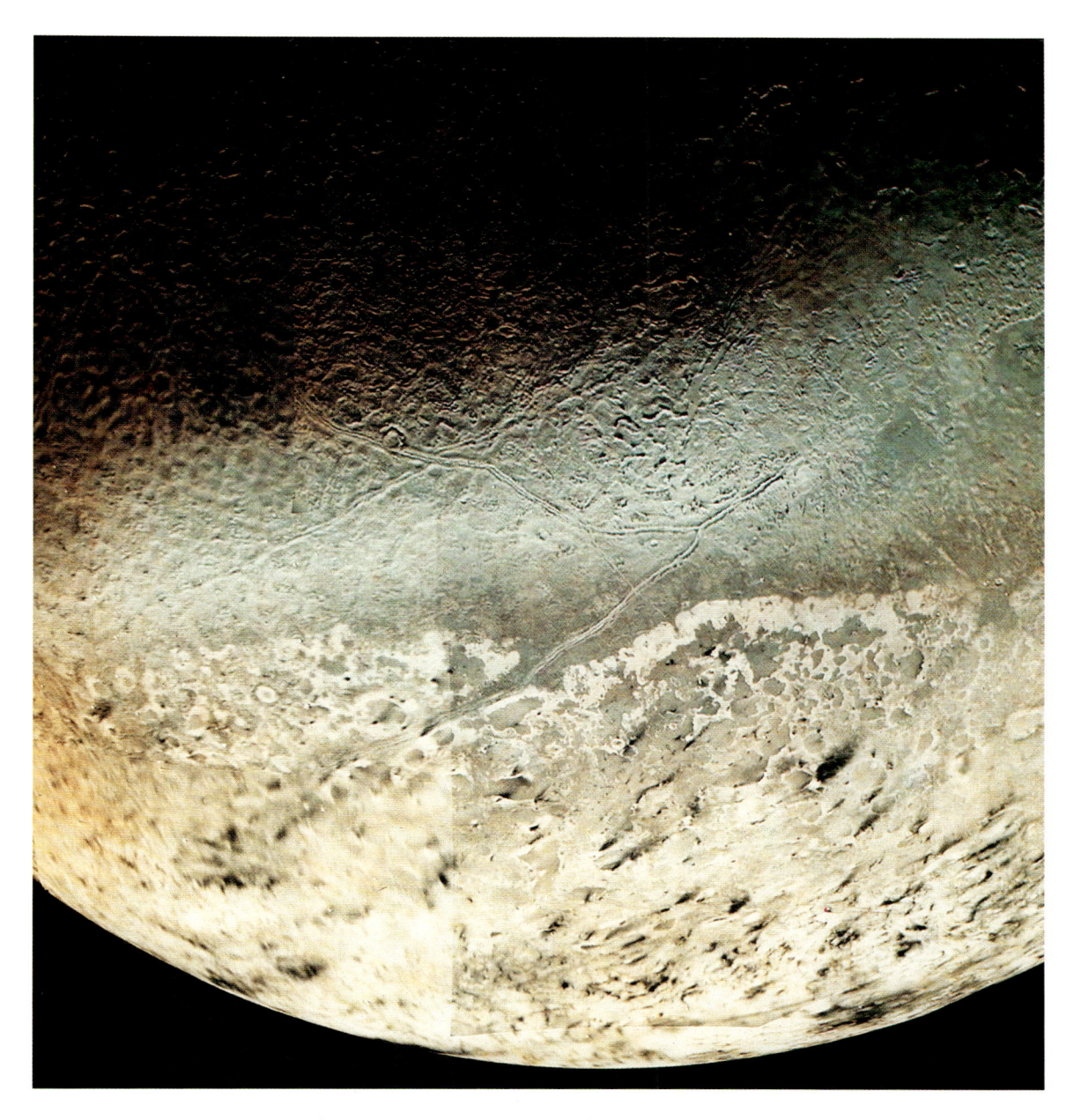

Triton's southern polar cap is a bright reflector of light. It is probably formed of nitrogen ice. To the north is a pale, bluish mottled region, etched across with long, ridge-sided canyons, darkening from blue to ruddy orange in the shadows beyond the sunlit side of the moon.

Cantaloup Melon in Space

Voyager swooped past Triton at a distance of 38,500 kilometres (23,925 miles) and transmitted pictures of such brilliance and detail that they made up for the lack of detail of the Neptune pictures. Triton's surface reveals evidence of a strange and complex geological history. There are relatively few cratered areas. One huge region north of the southern polar cap resembles the skin of a cantaloup melon. It is covered with roughly circular depressions, each one ringed with a ridge.

> **Did You Know?**
> Uranus and Neptune are smaller than Jupiter and Saturn but they are of similar composition. Together, they form a second pair of 'gas giants'.

Triton has extensive, basin-like areas surrounded by rocky tiers and cliffs of ice. The central basin in this picture has a diameter of 200 kilometres (125 miles). Triton is the coldest known object in the Solar System, and surface ice there is as hard as steel.

Through this mottled terrain, great canyon-like fissures cross and divide in enormous 'X' and 'Y' shapes. They are formed from parallel ridges a few hundred metres in height, outlining valleys up to 20 kilometres (12½ miles) across.

Great lake-like plains on Triton's surface are almost certainly made of deeply frozen water. These solid lakes are edged with tiers, which may have been formed by

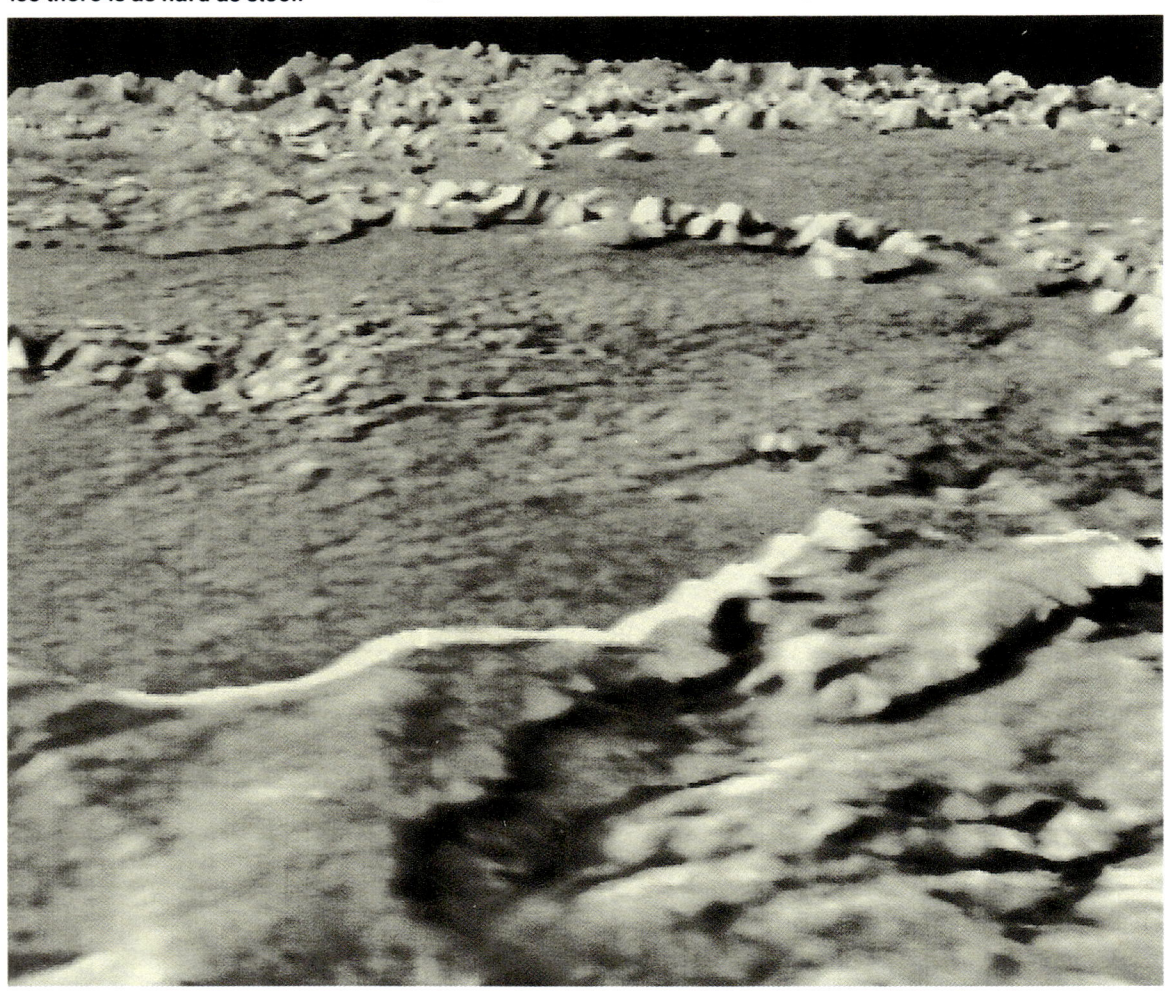

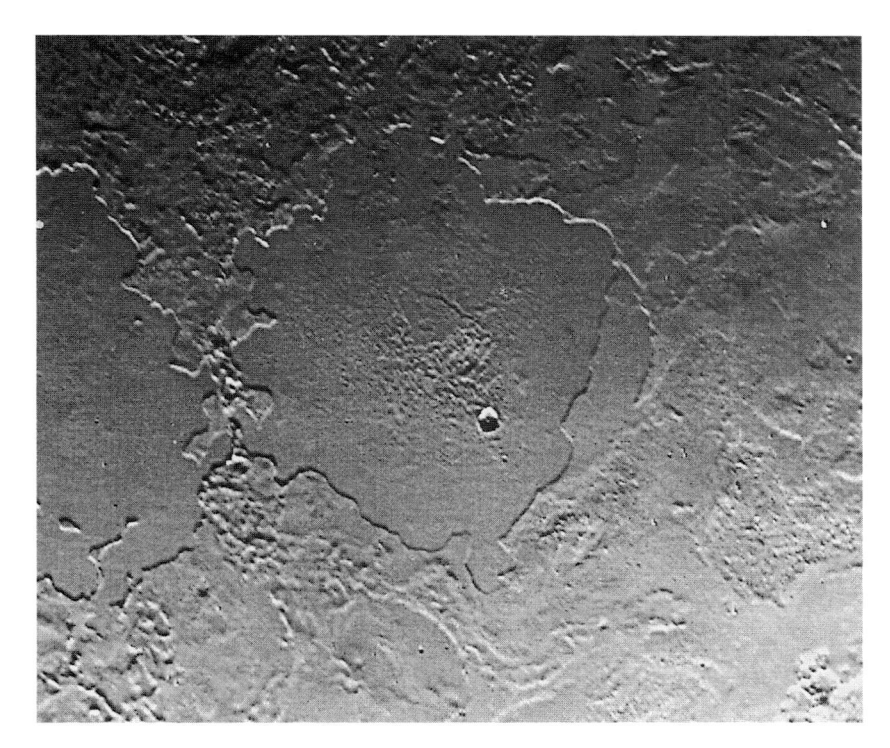

Some areas of Triton have smooth, enclosed, lake-like features, where low-temperature streams of water, ammonia, and methane have flowed from fissures to flood plains before being frozen to a steely hardness. These lakes often display fresh-looking craters.

Below: Neptune and its two major satellites (one arrowed immediately below the planet, one top right).

47

> ### Did You Know?
> Neptune appears at its brightest when viewed through telescopes on Earth during periods of minimum sunspot activity. During high sunspot activity, global hazes form around Neptune, affecting its apparent brightness as seen from Earth.

repeated melting and freezing. Only water would freeze rigidly enough to form these terraces, which can be half a mile high. Other available elements, such as methane and nitrogen, would flow like *glaciers* under their own weight.

Geysers of Triton

Triton was once very much hotter than it is now, and it is still volcanically active. Voyager images have revealed that *geysers* send regular jets 8 kilometres (5 miles) high into Triton's atmosphere. They are

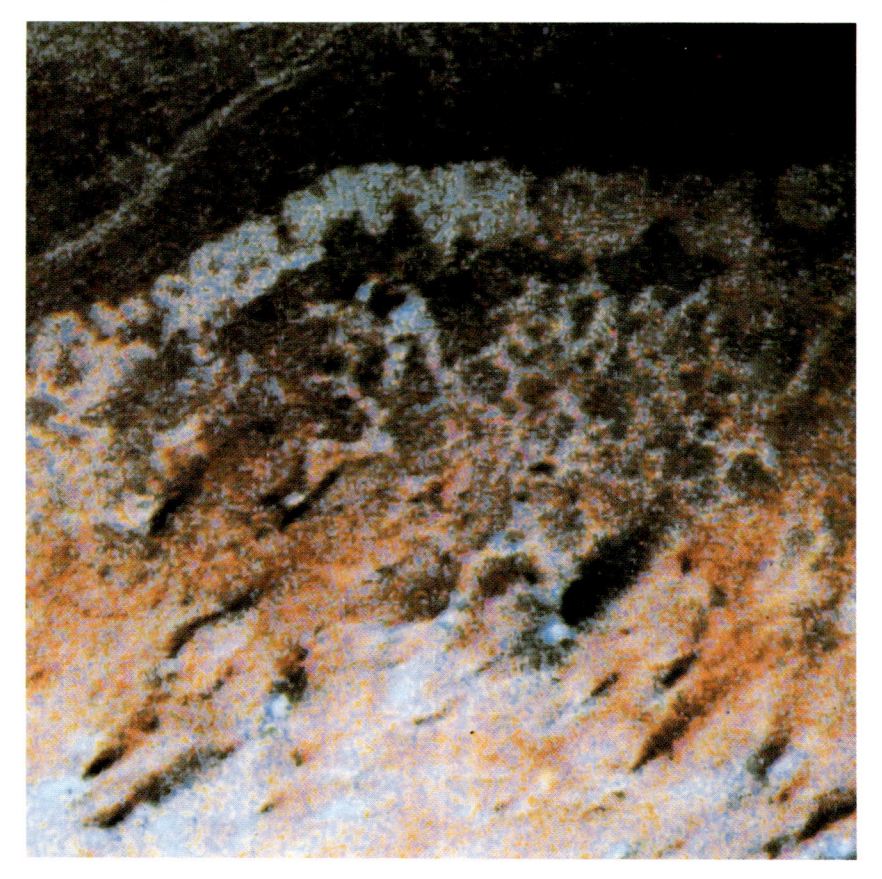

The dark streaking in this image of Triton may be the result of icy geysers, which are believed to send plumes of nitrogen ice and gas, together with sun-darkened methane ice crystals, high into the atmosphere. Winds blow the plumes across the moon's surface to form dark streaks up to 50 kilometres (30 miles) wide and 75 kilometres (45 miles) long.

> ### Did You Know?
> A human being living on Neptune would never live for one Neptune year. The Neptune year is the time it takes Neptune to travel once around the Sun – 165 Earth years.

caught by the planet's 300 km/h (200 mph) winds and carried downwind, showing up on Voyager's pictures as long dark smudges. The Voyager team believes that the most likely explanation for these geysers is subterranean heat that drives nitrogen and other elements up through underground fissures, where they burst explosively into the atmosphere. The nitrogen also carries crystals of sun-darkened methane. The winds carry them for miles before depositing them as dark streaks on Triton's surface. Triton thus joins Earth, Venus and Jupiter's Io as the only known bodies in the Solar System with current volcanic activity.

Triton orbits Neptune at a distance of 355,300 kilometres (220,000 miles), completing one orbit every 5·88 days. It was first seen by William Lassell in 1846, using a reflecting telescope that he built himself. It had a 60-centimetre (24-inch) mirror and was the largest reflecting telescope in England at the time.

Ancient Survivor

Triton may be a survivor from the period, more than four billion years ago, when the planets were mopping up the solar building blocks known as *planetesimals*. There are many similarities between Pluto and Triton, and some scientists believe that both were planetesimals that somehow avoided being

> ### Did You Know?
> Neptune is almost a twin of Uranus, but it is slightly smaller and does not have the strange tilt of Uranus.

> ## Did You Know?
> The temperature of Neptune's upper atmosphere has been measured as −216°C (−356·8°F). Because of its immense distance from the Sun, scientists had calculated that it would be colder. As Neptune continues to contract under its strong gravity field, 'excess heat' is produced as heavy molecules from the mantle settle downwards.

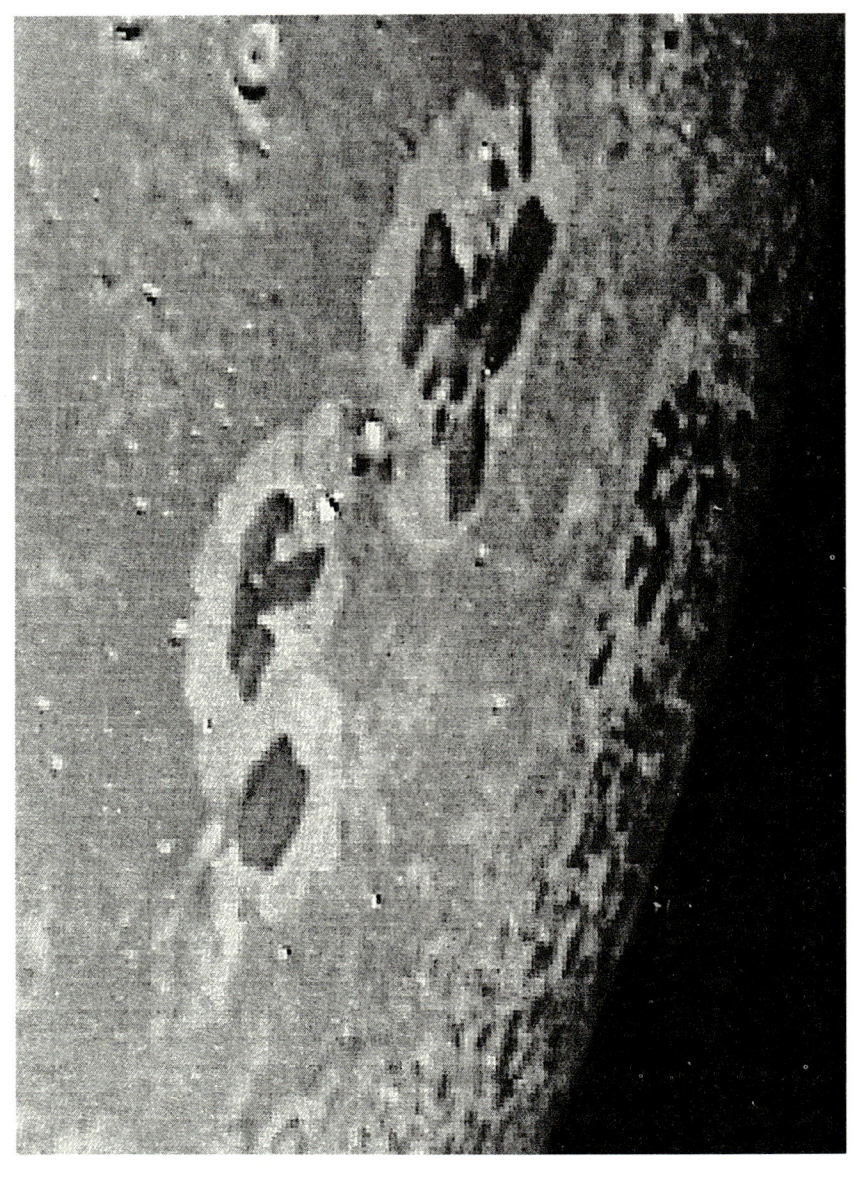

Patches of dark material rimmed with bright boundaries are visible on Triton's surface. They could be the result of material, including darkened methane, bubbling up from under the moon's crust.

absorbed into the bulk of the young Neptune. Perhaps they moved into orbit round the planet instead. In this orbit, following the rotation of the planet, both Triton and Pluto may have experienced enormous tidal flexing. It could have caused the internal heating that triggered Triton's geological formation. A heavy core of silicate minerals may have been created, and flows of melted material may have covered the surface, erasing many of the older impact craters and helping to mould Triton's current surface patterns.

The theory is that the orbits of Triton and Pluto were unstable, and that eventually they came too close to each other. Traumatic vibrations sent Pluto winging out of Neptune's grasp to take up its present eccentric orbit. Neptune's gravitational pull meanwhile held on to Triton, but only after orbital upsets that ended with its current retrograde path. Triton's orbit is still unstable: eventually, it will be pulled into the planet, to be broken up. Then it will probably join Neptune's small family of rings and tiny moons.

> ### Did You Know?
> Of all the giant planets, Neptune is the densest, with a density of 1·66 grams (0·6 ounce) per cubic centimetre. Jupiter has a greater mass, but is less compressed. Therefore, Neptune must contain a greater proportion of heavy elements.

End of an Era

The Triton fly-by marked the end of Voyager's Solar System task load. In some ways, the 12 years of its 'grand tour' were the most fruitful in the history of space information. Both probes are now headed for the edge of the Solar System. Electrical power and fuel sources may last until the year 2040. They will continue, barring accidents, to send back information to Earth about the far reaches of the Solar System, and even after they have become silent, they will journey on at a speed of 4·5 *Astronomical Units* (673,190,415 kilometres or 418,312,560 miles) a year through the Milky Way Galaxy for hundreds of thousands of years.

Pluto

Tiny Pluto, 5,900,000,000 kilometres (3,700,000,000 miles) from the Sun, has a diameter of a mere 2,300 kilometres (1,430 miles). It follows a lonely, extremely eccentric orbit that takes 248·5 years to complete. Unlike all the other known planets (except

Pluto, pictured here with its moon Charon, may once have been a planetesimal. It could have been trapped by Neptune's gravity like Triton, but released by some trauma, such as an interplanetary collision.

> **Pluto Facts**
> Average distance from Sun: 5,900 million km (3,700 million miles)
> Nearest distance from Earth: 5,800 million km (3,600 million miles)
> Average temperature (clouds): −150°C (−240°F)
> Diameter across equator: 2,300 km (1,430 miles)
> Atmosphere: None?
> Number of moons: 1 known
> Length of day: 6 days 9 hours
> Length of year: 248·5 Earth years

for Mercury), which have orbits varying very little from the plane of the ecliptic – the apparent path of the Sun across the sky – Pluto's orbit is at an angle of 17°10′ to the ecliptic. It forms a very extended oval, with an eccentricity of 0·246, while the other planets, again with the exception of Mercury, have almost circular orbits. At aphelion, Pluto is 7,400,000,000 kilometres (4,600,000,000 miles) from the Sun. At perihelion, it is as close as 4,600,000,000 kilometres (2,858,000,000 miles). For part of this eccentric orbit, Pluto moves inside the orbit of Neptune. So for some 20 years–1979 to 1999 in the current orbit–Neptune becomes, temporarily, the farthest known planet.

Right: Pluto was found by comparing photographic plates taken at the Lowell Observatory in Flagstaff, Arizona, where Percival Lowell had installed a succession of large refracting telescopes including this one, for planetary observations.

On the Trail Again

Pluto was discovered on 18 February 1930, as a dot on a photographic plate, after a search which had been going on since the discovery of Neptune in 1846. However, despite the systematic process that identified Pluto as a planet, it now appears, in the light of more recent information, that Pluto cannot have been the planet that was being sought.

Neptune was found by seeking the cause of

Even through the largest telescopes, Pluto appears like a small star. It is identified as a planet by its motion amongst the fixed stars as shown in these two photographs. The planet is arrowed in each picture.

irregularities in the orbit of Uranus. Scientists soon realized that there had been a considerable element of luck in finding Neptune. There were more irregularities in the orbit of Uranus than could be explained by the influence of Neptune. Therefore, there was a renewed search for another planet early in the twentieth century.

Two American astronomers, Percival Lowell, who had set up the Lowell Observatory in Flagstaff, Arizona, to pursue his theories about the canals of Mars, and William Pickering, who had helped him build it, started to calculate what kind of body to look for, and where to look. They conducted their searches independently, and in competition, as they had quarrelled since the old Flagstaff days.

Pickering was seeking 'Planet O', one that was twice as heavy as Earth. Lowell was looking for a much larger

> **Did You Know?**
> Pluto was discovered in 1930. With a diameter of 2,300 kilometres (1,430 miles) it is smaller than our Moon, making it the smallest and lightest planet in the Solar System.

body, a 'Planet X', seven times the weight of Earth. Lowell died in 1916, but the search was resumed at the Lowell Observatory with new funds and a new photographic telescope in 1927.

Clyde Hits the Jackpot

The Lowell Observatory employed an eager young amateur astronomer to help with photographing selected regions of sky and comparing the plates to see if one of the 'stars' had changed position. Young Clyde Tombaugh learned how to operate the instruments and embarked on a detailed search of the entire Zodiac. In 1930 Tombaugh found a minute, dim point of light that moved position when two plates, taken a few days apart, were compared. Clyde Tombaugh had become the third man in history to find a new planet.

Sorry, Wrong Planet

However, many astronomers, including Tombaugh himself, were puzzled by the find. It was certainly very close to the position in the heavens predicted by the complex calculations of Percival Lowell, and to one of the options calculated by William Pickering. The problem was its size. Both Lowell and Pickering had calculated that a planet with a mass much larger than Earth's was needed to explain the irregularities in Uranus's orbit not already accounted for by the presence of Neptune. Yet this new planet was so tiny that, despite very high magnification, it remained an insignificant point of light. Unless it possessed an unheard-of density, higher than that of lead, it could not be responsible for affecting the orbits of gas giants like Uranus and Neptune.

Pluto's Running Mate

In 1978, confirmation came that Pluto was not super-dense. At the U.S. Naval Observatory in Washington, D.C., an astronomer named Jim Christy was studying

> ### Did You Know?
> For most of the time, Pluto is the furthest planet from Earth. An aircraft travelling at a speed of 1,810 km/h (1,125 mph) would take about 370 years to travel from Earth to Pluto.

photographic plates taken with a new telescope in Arizona, not far from Lowell Observatory. On the plates, Pluto's image was elongated, and the plates had been put aside because they were thought to be defective. Christy noticed that star images on the same

Percival Lowell built the observatory that bears his name in Arizona. Lowell died in 1916, but his research to find Planet X was resumed with a new photographic telescope in 1927. Pluto was found in 1930. This wide-angle view shows the original 60-centimetre (24-inch) refracting telescope used by Lowell. The pink spot visible through the open shutter is the planet Mars.

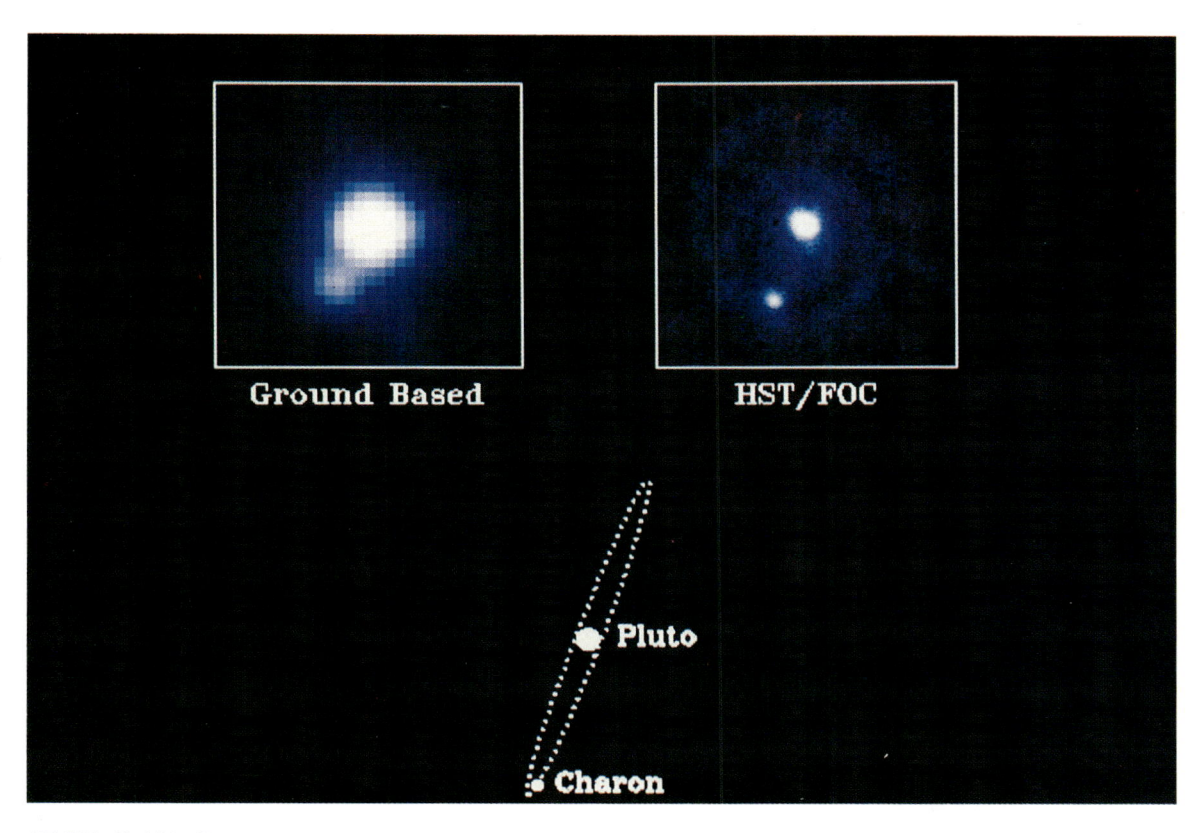

NASA's Hubble Space Telescope obtained the clearest pictures ever of Pluto and its moon Charon. In this illustration the picture in the right hand box is the one taken by the faint object camera. This is the first long duration Hubble Telescope photograph taken of a moving object. The picture in the left hand box shows a picture taken from Earth. The diagram at the bottom shows Charon's orbit round Pluto. It is a circle seen nearly end on from Earth.

plates were sharp. There could not be a fault in the machinery. Christy realized that Pluto's 'elongation' revealed the presence of a large moon. Study of plates taken years earlier confirmed Christy's find. The moon was christened 'Charon', Pluto's ferryman in classical mythology.

Double Act

Calculations soon showed that Charon orbited Pluto at a distance of nearly 20,000 kilometres (12,500 miles), every 6.4 days. It was now possible to use a well-established mathematical relationship to calculate the combined mass of Pluto and Charon. Together, they were

---

Did You Know?
Pluto's moon Charon, is named after the character in Greek mythology who was a ferryman in the realm of Pluto. It was a happy coincidence for Jim Christy, its discoverer, that the name was so like that of his wife Charlene.

57

only a small fraction – about one five-hundredth – of the mass of Earth. There was no way that they could influence Uranus or Neptune. Tombaugh's discovery had been a remarkable coincidence, and the elusive 'Planet X' remains to be found.

Opposite: **If Planet X does exist, information sent back to Earth by the IRAS spacecraft will identify it amongst over half a million sources of heat it recorded in the sky. The supercooled IRAS would have found any heat emitted by any planet beyond Neptune and Pluto. No one has so far picked out evidence of Planet X from the data.**

Right: **Pioneer 10 has passed all the planets. If there is a Planet X beyond Neptune and Pluto any gravitational pull will be felt by Pioneer if the planet is in the vicinity of the spacecraft.**

As seen from Pluto, Charon would seem to hang motionless in the same part of the sky all the time. The planet and its moon are locked in position with the same face turned towards each other all the time. They rotate around a mutual centre of gravity and should perhaps be considered a double planet, as Charon has a diameter of 1,186 kilometres (736 miles), more than half that of Pluto. It is the largest satellite, relative to the size of the planet it orbits, in the Solar System.

Cold and Rocky

Pluto is now known to have a density just over twice that of water, indicating that it contains a rocky core. This centre is probably overlaid with a mantle of frozen water and methane. The planet has a thin atmosphere, and the surface pressure is less than one hundred-thousandth that of Earth. The atmosphere probably consists of methane in gaseous form, together with heavy gases such as nitrogen, argon, carbon monoxide and oxygen. The surface temperature is around $-216°C$ ($-355°F$).

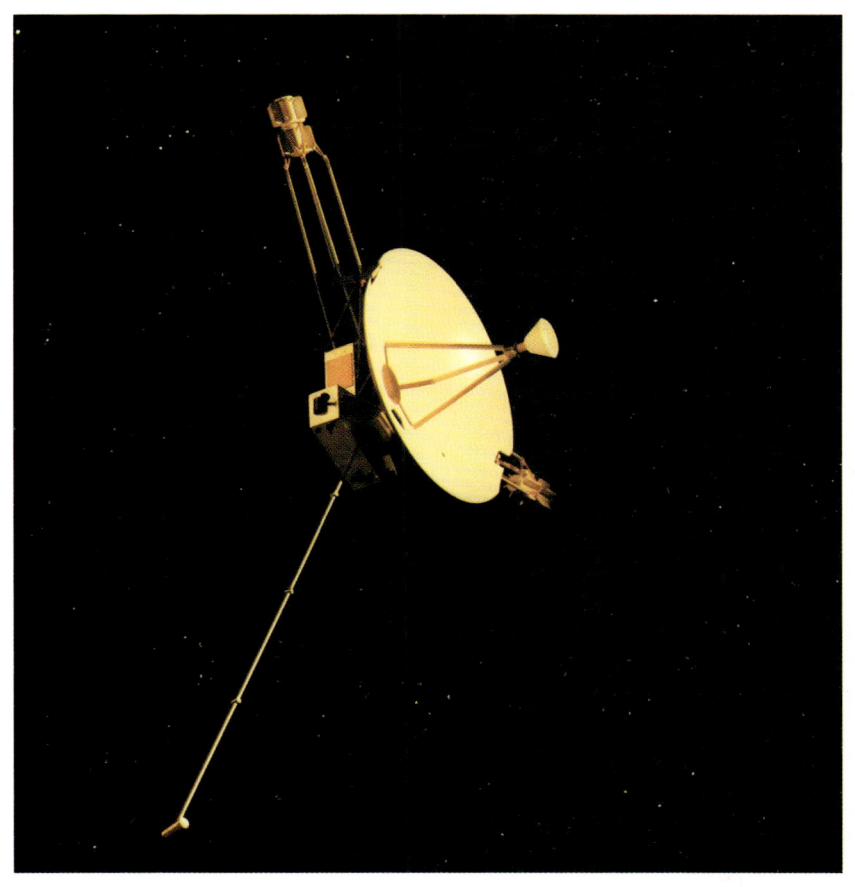

Like Uranus, Pluto is turned over in relation to its orbital plane, pursuing its far-ranging, centuries-long orbit with its spin axis tilted at an angle of 122°.

Where Do We Go From Here?

Voyager was not able to rendezvous with Pluto. That makes it the only known planet in the Solar System not to have been visited by human technology. The flight time to Pluto from Earth is fourteen years, but it is certain that our curiosity will not allow us to rest until we have had a closer look at our least-known fellow planet. Meanwhile, the irregularities in the orbits of both Uranus and Neptune remain to be fully explained. The search for the mysterious 'tenth planet' continues.

NASA's Deep Space Network in California receives the faintest signals from Pioneer 10 as it goes deeper into space. The giant 64-metre (210 foot) antenna will be able to track the spacecraft until it is twice as far away from Earth as Pluto is.

Books to Read

Astronomy Peter Lafferty (Cherrytree Books, 1989)
The Cambridge Guide to the Earth David Lambert (Cambridge University Press, 1988)
The Mysterious Universe Nigel Henbest (Ebury Press, 1981)
The Kingdom of the Sun Isaac Asimov (Collier, 1962)
Galaxies (Time-Life, 1989)
The Moon Patrick Moore (Mitchell Beazley, 1981)
Exploring the Universe Protheroe/Capriotti/Newson (Merrill Publishing Co., 1989)
The Illustrated History of NASA Robin Kerrod (Prion, 1986)
Horizons – Exploring the Universe Michael A. Seeds (Wadsworth Publishing Co., 1989)
The Greenwich Guide to Stars, Galaxies and Nebulae Stuart Malin (George Philip/National Maritime Museum, 1989)
The Greenwich Guide to the Planets Stuart Malin (George Philip/National Maritime Museum, 1989)
The Planets Peter Francis (Pelican Books, 1981)
The Planets Heather Couper/Nigel Henbest (Pan/Channel Four, 1985)
Exploration of the Solar System William J. Kaufmann III (Macmillan Publishing Co. N.Y., 1978)
Solar System Peter Ryan/Ludek Pesek (Allen Lane, 1978)
Pathways to the Universe Francis Graham-Smith/Bernard Lovell (Cambridge University Press, 1988)
The Universe and the Earth Ardley/Ridpath/Harben (Macdonald Educational, 1978)
Apollo Robin Scagell (Prion, 1989)

Glossary

APHELION The farthest point from the Sun of any object in solar orbit.

ASTRONOMICAL UNIT (AU) A unit of measurement used for Solar System distances, equal to the average distance of Earth from the Sun, about 93 million miles (150 million kilometres).

CIRRUS CLOUD Wispy, high-altitude clouds, usually consisting of ice crystals.

COMPASS BEARING A directional line determined by the use of a magnetic compass and map.

DEEP INTERIOR ROTATION RATE The basic rate of rotation of a gaseous planet or satellite, as opposed to the apparent, or differential, rotation rates of its atmospheric gases.

DENSITY The mass of a substance per unit of volume, measured, for example, in grams per cubic centimetre.

DOUBLE STAR A pair of stars which appear from Earth to be close together.

DYNAMIC ATMOSPHERE An atmosphere constantly in motion, driven by cyclical climatic forces, powered in turn by solar or internal heating.

GEYSER An intermittent jet of boiling water, mud or steam, which shoots up powered by subterranean heat and pressure.

GLACIER A slowly flowing body of ice.

IMPACT CRATER A crater in the surface of a planet or satellite caused by the fall of a meteorite.

JET PROPULSION LABORATORY (JPL) Mission control center in California where U.S. planetary space probes are monitored.

MAGNETIC NORTH The northern pole of the Earth's magnetic field, which attracts compass needles. Its direction varies from that of the true north of the spin axis.

MILKY WAY A dense ribbon of stars that marks the flattened plane of our galaxy.

MILKY WAY GALAXY The star system to which our solar system belongs.

NEBULA (NEBULAE) A dusty, gaseous cloud in interstellar space.

OCCULT/OCCULTATION A phenomenon that occurs when one celestial body moves in front of and masks another as seen from Earth.

OPTICS The study of the properties and behaviour of light.

PERIHELION The closest point of an object in solar orbit to the Sun.

PLANETESIMAL One of the tiny bodies formed in the early stages of the Solar System that were the building blocks of the planets.

ROYAL GREENWICH OBSERVATORY An astronomical observatory founded by King Charles II in 1675. Sited originally in Greenwich, near London, the observatory was established mainly for navigational purposes.